MW00617943

Guided Meditations for Adult Catechumens

Sydney Ann Merritt

Resource Publications, Inc.
San Jose, California

Reprint Department
Resource Publications, Inc.
160 E. Virginia Street #290
San Jose, CA 95112-5876
1-408-286-8505 (voice)
1-408-287-8748 (fax)

Library of Congress Cataloging-in-Publication Data
Merritt, Sydney Ann.
    Guided meditations for adult catechumens / Sydney Ann Merritt.
      p.   cm.
    ISBN 0-89390-452-X (pbk.)
     1. Catechumens—Prayer—books and devotions—English.
    2. Catholic Church—Prayer—books and devotions—English.
    I. Title.
    BX2170.C38M47   1999
    242—dc21   98-52094

Printed in the United States of America

99 00 01 02 03 I 5 4 3 2 1

Editorial director: Nick Wagner
Prepress manager: Elizabeth J. Asborno
Production coordinator: Mike Sagara
Copyeditor: Robin Witkin

The Scripture quotations contained herein are from the New Revised Standard Version of the Bible, copyrighted, 1989 by the Division of the Christian Education of the National Council of the Churches of Christ in the United States of America, and are used by permission. All rights reserved.

To my mother, Louise Ross,
a model of perfection in the ways of
a mother and grandmother,
and to my father, Howard Ross,
who taught me to love the written word.
Thank you both so much for sharing your love with me.
I still feel your presence in all that I do
and in all those I love.

Contents

Part 3:
Period of Purification and Enlightenment

Part 4:
Period of Postbaptismal Catechesis or Mystagogy

Acknowledgments

Thank you to all who loved and encouraged me during this project; Lee, my husband of so many years, and Father Dan Reynolds who shared his wisdom and love, a priest who taught me what a pastor really is.

Teaching Adult Catechumens To Experience Jesus Through Guided Meditation

The meditations and reflections found in this book are an effective method of teaching adult catechumens how to experience Jesus within their minds and hearts. The meditations follow the entire catechumenate process including the inquiry period through mystagogy. Meditations, reflections, prayers, and activities that are based on the rites are written for cycle A, following the outline for Christian Initiation of Adults. You will also find many meditations, discussion questions, and prayers that follow the lectionary readings for cycles A, B, and C. At the beginning of each meditation, I list the related Scripture citations, Sunday and season (with cycle[s] indicated in parentheses), and suggested background music. The book also includes retreat reflections based on the readings for the Easter vigil.

This book provides the opportunity for adults to awaken their imaginations, establishing a place where they may meet with Jesus. Meditations and reflections will lead them to their own experience of Jesus and spirituality. Adults are led into the Gospel scene where they will encounter the Lord through touch, feel, love, and prayer. They will "hear" the brush of angel's wings, "feel" the chilling waters of the Jordan River, and "hear" the call of Jesus across the stormy sea.

The meditations can be merged into any catechumenate program or retreat. For those who use CELEBRATING THE LECTIONARY from Resource Publications, Inc., you can incorporate the meditations into your weekly lesson plans as an alternate activity or use them as introductions or conclusions to a unit.

Discussion questions follow each meditation. I do not suggest inviting the adults to share their own experience of the meditations because this should remain a personal time with Jesus. However, if they volunteer to share a portion of their experiences, you will find that it stimulates the discussion time.

Scripture quotations are taken from the New Revised Standard Version or are my paraphrase of Scripture.

Suggestions for Success

Teaching the catechumens to experience Jesus through prayer should be rewarding for the presenter as well. Following a few simple suggestions will help to ensure your success.

To Begin

Begin with "The Meeting Place," the introductory guided meditation found at the end of this introduction. This will create a place in their imaginations to meet Jesus.

Personal Reflection

Before presenting a meditation, take a few minutes for your personal reflection on the Gospel scene. What images quicken your imagination? Ask yourself, "What is Jesus saying to me?"

Practice

To help you become more comfortable with this form of prayer, practice reading the meditation aloud slowly just as you will with the group. You may choose to record and play back the meditation, listening for pauses and voice inflection. Are you speaking too softly or too quickly? Are your words clear? Are you pausing long enough?

- Read slowly with slight pauses where indicated (....). A count of four works well. For longer pauses, wait one to three minutes or until you notice they are becoming restless.

- Avoid speaking in a monotone. Change your voice to emphasize a change in character or scene.

- When reading the Gospel or familiarizing them with prayer during sessions, find creative ways to share the word. For example, try divided group readings in which one side of the group reads every other verse or portion of prayer aloud. For longer readings you may wish to try assigning voices of the main characters in the reading, such as a male taking the part of Jesus or one of the disciples, a female taking the part of Mary, the Woman at the Well, etc. Prayers said in an echo format are also beautiful, for example:

> Leader: Glory be to the Father.
> Second Voice: Glory be to the Father.
> Third Voice: ... to the Father.
>
> Leader: And to the Son.
> Second Voice: And to the Son.
> Third Voice: ... to the Son.

Music

Background music is very important; it sets the tone and helps activate the imagination. You will find music suggestions at the beginning of each meditation. (See "Music Resources" for the listing of suggested recorded music.) Don't be afraid to experiment with your own favorite instrumentals. Most important be sure the rhythm is constant. Don't let the rhythm drag, and watch out for abrupt changes in the instruments or timing. Live music and sounds—soft guitar, gentle piano music, tinkling wind chimes—can also be helpful.

Space

Give some thought to how you will create an atmosphere of prayer for adults.

- Lower the lights or pull the shades.
- Use a candle.
- Create a focal point by combining important elements: a cruciform; an open Bible; a candle; natural objects like rocks, driftwood, or greenery; a crucifix or cross.

Make sure the catechumens will be physically comfortable. If the chairs are hard and narrow, it will be more difficult. Some adults may prefer lying on the carpet rather than sitting at a desk or in a wooden chair. Attempt to provide space between each person. Floor pillows are a great way of indicating private space.

Discussion

Allow time for discussion questions. Invite responses, but do not demand participation. Stress that in most cases there is no wrong or right answer; the answer is based on how they "feel" about a subject or how they imagine the outcome. Introspective questions should be done in a small group or during the prayer time.

Prayer

There are suggestions for closing prayers. This is a very necessary element that brings meaningful closure to the session. Invite participation through prayer petitions or assign a group to design a closing prayer for the next session. This also builds community bonds.

Keep Trying

Do not become discouraged if your first attempts are not what you hoped for. Even your first awkward tries will have an impact. Each person will take home something personal and different. You *can* do it!

The Meeting Place

Suggested Music: "Peace Is Flowing Like a River"/*Gentle Sounds*

> *I, the light, have come into the world,*
> *so that whoever believes in me shall remain in*
> *the darkness no longer (Jn 8:12).*

My days are hectic with responsibility. There is barely time for
me. Where does God fit into this picture? Many times, God
takes a back seat to my family and my job. Praying should be
a simple act—just talking to God while I'm on the move if that
is the only time I have. My shower often becomes my personal
"prayer closet," offering privacy and time with him. At night,
waiting for sleep to release me from the busy day, I lie awake
listening for his voice. One of my children put the difficulty of
conversations with God into perspective for me. She said, "I
could sure talk to God a lot easier if I could just see him.
Sometimes I think that I may be just talking to the walls."

There is a way that we can see Jesus. It is with that wonderful
phenomenon called *imagination*. As a child, you had plenty
of it. You just need to wake it up again. Meditation is an
ancient prayer form, one undoubtedly used by our Lord.

What was your favorite childhood game that used your
imagination? Did you always go to a special place? If you
could use your imagination now to meet our Lord, where
would you meet him? (*Invite participation.*) Let's give it a try.

Meditation

Find a comfortable position .... Close your eyes .... Shut away
the sounds of the day .... Forget the tensions nagging at

you .... Allow your body to feel heavy and limp .... Take a deep breath .... Let it out slowly .... Whisper "Jesus" ....

Imagine a lazy summer day with nothing to do .... Perhaps you are walking down a dusty path, a road to nowhere in particular ....

Around the next bend nod to the man standing by the side of the road .... His long hair is swept back from his suntanned face .... The hem of his garment is stained from the red, claylike soil .... In the background, you hear water washing against the sandy shore .... The man looks at you and smiles .... Can you see him? .... He turns to face you .... He is familiar, but .... It is Jesus! .... "Where are you going, Lord?" you ask .... Jesus smiles once again. Taking your hand in his, he says, "Come, follow me. I, the light, have come into the world, so that whoever believes in me need not remain in the dark anymore. I promise you light where there has been darkness" ....

You and Jesus walk hand-in-hand toward the water .... Jesus rests for a moment against a small tree, his back leaning against its bark .... Jesus turns away slowly to look toward the blue-green lake .... He invites you to walk with him to the water's edge .... Be careful going down the sloping hillside .... "Don't fall," Jesus cautions .... Jesus removes his well-worn sandals, walking into the cool water .... He slowly bends forward, forming a cup with his hands .... Then dipping his hands into the water, he offers you a drink .... Place your hands over his .... Drink in the cool, fresh water .... Jesus bends forward, picking up a small flat rock .... He throws it into the air .... The rock lands almost without a splash, then skips across the lake .... Jesus hands you a rock, challenging your expertise .... You and Jesus chuckle .... Throw the rock like a discus .... Delightfully, nearly invisible rings appear on the surface of the water .... The flat rock skips and jumps through each hoop .... Jesus laughs, then raises his hand, forming a circle with his thumb and index finger .... "Pretty good, my friend"....

Now it is your turn. Take Jesus by the hand, leading him to your favorite place ....

Tall trees line the path, reaching their arms to the heavens .... Take a deep breath .... The air smells sweet of fresh grass and rose blossoms .... Look up at the sky .... Clouds drift across the face of the sun .... A warm breeze blows his long, dark hair .... You have now arrived at your special place .... It may be at home, in a park, high in the mountains, or at a sandy beach .... You can be with Jesus wherever you want to be .... Invite Jesus to sit down .... Take a seat beside him or perhaps in the safety of his lap .... No one will see you .... Be where you are comfortable .... Feel the security of his arms folding around you .... Feel his love .... You are now alone with Jesus in your favorite place ....

I will give you a few moments to be alone with Jesus .... Speak to him quietly in your heart .... Ask him anything you want .... Talk to him .... Tell him all those things that may be on your heart .... The light of Christ shines upon you .... Jesus whispers, "At this time, what do you ask of me, my child?" (*Pause until they grow restless.*)

Prayer

Jesus, I have found you in my resting place. A place to talk, a place to be myself before you. May I always be aware of your presence in my life, guiding, protecting, and loving. I place my life in your hands. May your light remove shadows from my life. Amen.

Jesus stands with his hands outstretched above your head, offering this blessing, "Lord God, strengthen this child in faith, that all may know you, the one true God, and your Son whom you have sent. Amen."

It is time for you to leave .... Jesus offers you a warm embrace .... "Good-bye for now," he says .... Turn and walk away .... Wave good-bye .... Walk down the sandy path .... Open your eyes and return to this room.

Discussion

- What did you see? What did your hear?
- What qualities would you use to describe Jesus?

Optional: This may be a good time to ask the group to share the first word that comes to mind when you say, "Jesus."

Part 1

Period Of Evangelization And Precatechumenate

We Begin Our Journey Of Faith

*Lord, surround us in your love and mercy
as we place our trust in you.*

Scripture: Genesis 12:1–4a

"And in the beginning God made man in his likeness—and God was pleased." In the passing centuries of time human beings came to worship many false gods. They fell upon their knees in times of honor and of sorrow to the gods manifesting themselves in the wind and weather, in the crops, in the sun in the sky, and in the time of great happiness. But they did not know our God. At long last, Abram and Sarai received *the call* from God to leave everything behind and enter into a covenant with him. In answer to this call from God, Abram and Sarai begin their own journey of faith: to find the identity of God. This is our journey of faith also.

Abram and Sarai *listened* to the voice of God, their first act of faith. Take a moment to reflect on God's promise to Abram:

I will bless those who bless you and curse those who curse you; and the entire world will be blessed because of you.

You, too, have heard the call of God …. God's blessings and promise to Abram are also for you …. The blessings of God are upon you.

(Pause for reflection.) The entire world will be blessed because of you.

Brief Discussion

- Is it difficult for you to accept the responsibility of God's blessing?
- What message did you hear?
- How does God speak to you?

We Have Found The Messiah

Scripture: Jn 1:35–42
Celebration: Rite of Acceptance
Music Suggestion: "By Name I Have Called You"/*Gentle Sounds*

History has equated our faith process as a "journey of faith." Perhaps you have been on this journey since early childhood with a few detours along the way, or you may be taking your first steps. The Easter Vigil Mass will not signal the end of the road; the journey of faith is never complete.

John the Baptist heard the call of God. He knew that his mission was to announce the coming of the Messiah. John lived in faith upon the Scripture of Isaiah the prophet, "When you see the Holy Spirit descending and resting upon someone—he is the one you are looking for. He will baptize with the Holy Spirit." John baptized in water to point Jesus out to the nation of Israel.

John stood waist high in the waters of the Jordan River baptizing all who came forward. Near the end of the day, Our Lord stepped before John. As Scripture prophesied, the clouds parted, the voice of God spoke, and the Holy Spirit descended in the form of a dove. Jesus was the Messiah!

Let us awaken our imaginations to join John and two of his disciples the following day.

Meditation

Find a comfortable position .... Close your eyes .... Shut out the sounds and cares of the day .... Draw in a deep breath ....

Slowly exhale .... Allow relaxation to cover you like a warm
blanket on a cold winter's night .... Take a deep breath ....
Exhale .... Whisper "Jesus" ....

It is midday .... Momentarily, the sun dangles lazily
overhead .... You, John, and two of his disciples, yet unknown
to you, gather near the town of Bethany on the opposite side
of the Jordan River .... You sip water from a gourd .... Water
spills from your lips, dripping down your chin .... Offer water
to John .... He is a strange man, different in his dress and his
mission in life .... John's hair lies in long tangled locks .... His
eyes are dark in color, alive with Spirit ....

It is time to continue to Bethany .... John pats you on the
back, "You'll make it, friend" .... The other two men chuckle
quietly .... A man is approaching from the right roadway ....
He is not as tall as John, his hair is swept to the back and tied
neatly with a leather thong .... John squints in the bright
sunlight .... "There he is! There is Jesus!" John shouts ....
In John's excitement he grabs you by the arm, turning you
around .... He points emphatically, "There is the lamb of
God!" ....

Look down the road .... Place your hand above your eyes to
shield them from the glare of heat waves rising in the air ....
Can you see the lamb of God, known as Jesus? .... John's two
disciples speak not a word but immediately turn and follow
Jesus .... You quicken your steps to follow also .... Is your
response one of curiosity or faith? (Pause briefly.)

Jesus looks back over his shoulder to see the two strangers
and you following closely at his heels .... "What do you want?"
he asks .... Noticing you, Jesus smiles and takes your hand in
his in a gesture of welcome .... One of the men, short and
square in stature, pushes in beside Jesus ...."Where do you
live?" he demands .... Quickly, the second disciple chimes in,
"Where are you going?" ....

Jesus puts his arm loosely around your shoulders and resumes
walking .... Jesus calls back over his shoulders to the disciples,
"Come and see" .... The men quickly fall in behind you and
Jesus, nearly walking on your heels .... The journey takes you

13

by the riverside .... Nearly deserted except for two small fishing boats .... Gulls dip overhead, signaling a fresh load of fish .... The ground is hard .... Particles of sandy soil cover your feet .... Four hours dissolve into late afternoon .... The disciples ask many questions about the kingdom of God and about Jesus' identity .... The shorter man asks, "When will you begin your reign?" .... Jesus looks at you and smiles, "Sooner than you think" .... Afternoon fades into evening .... You light a campfire .... It hisses and spews clouds of smoke into the night air .... The second disciple, more reserved and younger, offers you a smoked fish from his satchel .... "My name is Andrew. I fish these waters often with my brother, Simon Peter. Perhaps you know of him." .... You gasp in surprise .... Jesus nods knowingly, then speaks to you, "These men shall be known to many" .... Andrew excuses himself to search for his brother, bringing him the news of the day, "We have found the Messiah!"

You and Jesus speak of many things in the waiting hours of evening .... Quiet covers the night .... Awaiting Andrew's return, Jesus invites you to walk with him .... A lone, barren tree looms in the shadows .... Jesus guides you to take a seat beneath the old tree .... Leaning against its ragged trunk, Jesus takes your hands in his .... "You shall stand before the body of my Church to answer questions that lie heavily upon my mind" .... Jesus grasps a limb of the tree, pulling himself to his feet .... He returns your gaze, then questions, "What do you ask of God?" .... Reflect in time. (*Pause.*) Jesus walks nearer, placing his hand on your shoulder, "What do you ask of my Church?" (*Pause.*) Jesus listens intently .... Jesus slowly paces back and forth, then stops to take your hands in his .... "God has called you. Your name is written upon the sands of time" .... Jesus stands on your right side, still holding your hand in his .... "God sends me to announce all that I have seen and heard, the mysteries of heaven and earth. Always try to pattern your life on the teachings of the word of God .... Are you ready to follow me—to live this life?" Jesus asks. (Pause.)

Jesus looks off into the distance. For a moment a shadow of sadness covers his face .... He continues, "I shall be known by my cross. I offer you this sign of your new way of life as a catechumen" .... Jesus helps you to your feet, placing his hand on your forehead .... You feel the trace of his cross.... "Receive the cross. It is I who now strengthens you with this sign of love .... Learn to know me and follow my path" .... Gently, he touches your ears, "Receive the sign of the cross on your ears, that you may hear my voice" .... You feel an awakening within .... The strength of the Lord is with you! .... Jesus traces the cross on your lips .... "That you may respond to the word of God" .... "Receive this sign upon your heart, that I may dwell there" .... The hand of Jesus touches each of your shoulders, "Bear my gentle yoke" .... Taking both of your hands in his, Jesus silently places your hands palm up .... He traces the cross in the center of each hand .... "May I be known in the work you do." .... Jesus bends down .... Taking the hem of his garment, he first wipes the sand from your feet, then traces each with the cross .... "May you walk in the way of the Lord" ....

Jesus holds his hands above your head .... Warmth flows through your body .... Jesus traces the sign of the cross above your head .... "I sign you with eternal life in the name of the Father, and of the Son, and of the Holy Spirit."*....

I will leave you alone with Jesus .... Take this time to talk with him .... Listen for his gentle voice. (*Pause.*)

Prayer

Father God, by the cross and resurrection of your Son, you have given life to your people. May I come to the glory of rebirth in baptism. May I persevere in the footsteps of Christ. Amen.

It is nearly time for you to leave .... Jesus holds you within his arms .... Peter, the brother of Andrew, watches from a distance .... Jesus continues to hold you .... Looking over your shoulder at Peter, he speaks, "He shall be known as Peter, the rock!" .... Turn to walk away .... Peter now stands before

* cf. RCIA 54–56

Jesus, his ragged red beard somehow out of place .... The path is washed in light .... A light from beyond the skies .... Walk down the path .... Open your eyes and return to this room.

Discussion

- What did you see? What did you hear?
- What was it about Jesus that drew you to him?
- Simon's name in Hebrew translates as "sinking sand." Jesus renamed him Peter, which meant "the rock."
- Why do you think Jesus made this change?
- If you were to pick a name for yourself that would describe where you feel you are at spiritually, what would it be?

Closing Prayer

Dim the lights, using one large candle. Play background music. Select three readers beforehand. Allow time for practice.

- Reader One: Psalms 33:4–5
- Reader Two: Psalms 33:12–13
- Reader Three: Psalms 33:18–19 20,22

Response following each verse: Happy the People the Lord
        has chosen to be his own.

Readings: RCIA 62

Leader: Lord,
        look with love on your servants,
        who commit themselves to your name
        and bow before you in worship.

        Help them to accomplish what is good;
        arouse their hearts, that they may always
        remember your works and your commands
        and eagerly embrace all that is yours.
        Grant this through Christ our Lord. Amen.

Part 2

Period Of The Catechumenate

Notes on Meditations During the Period of the Catechumenate

The meditations included here serve to nurture and develop the catechumens' faith and conversion to God. The readings come from all three cycles and the seasons of the church year. I have indicated the topic in the title. They will include topics studied during the period following the rite of acceptance through the Easter Vigil Mass.

Jesus Calls Your Name

Scripture: Mt 4:12–23; Mk 1:14–20
Feast: 3rd Sunday in Ordinary Time (AB)
Music Suggestion: any selection from *The Sea*
or "By Name I Have Called You"/*Gentle Sounds*

When Jesus first spoke with the four fishermen, they understood little of the task ahead. Undoubtedly, they knew little, if anything, about Jesus or his mission. Would they have joined him knowing what was ahead? Perhaps not. What would it take for you to walk away from your life to follow a perfect stranger?

The four fishermen heard Jesus calling. They answered his call. Jesus now calls your name. What will your answer be?

Release your imagination to slip into the time of our Lord. He awaits you near the Sea of Galilee.

Meditation

Find a comfortable position .... Close your eyes .... Allow your body to relax .... Shut out the sounds and cares of the day .... Allow relaxation to cover you like a warm blanket .... Take a deep breath .... Exhale. Whisper "Jesus" ....

You are walking on a sandy beach by the Sea of Galilee .... Time stands still as you await the return of Jesus .... Seawater slides in across the sand, leaving wet fingerprints upon the shore .... Gentle waves of water splash your legs .... Seaweed wraps around your feet .... Smell the freshness of the air .... The shore is deserted except for two small fishing vessels .... Seabirds circle overhead .... Can you hear their call? .... As you walk, wet sand curls around your toes .... With the next tide your footsteps will wash into the sea .... Two fishermen

19

sit by their boat, rolling a heavy net .... They have long beards, broad shoulders, and hands rough with callouses .... They talk happily as they work ....

Look out across the water .... A small craft bobs upon the sea...The fisherman waves .... Peer into the mist of the water .... You recognize the boat and the man .... It is Jesus! .... He calls your name .... Listen! .... Do you hear his call? .... The sound of your name echoes across the sea, bouncing off the hillside .... Jesus climbs over the side of boat, smiles, and reaches out to take your hand in greeting .... "Thank you for coming to meet me," Jesus says, giving you a pat on the shoulder .... "Come, follow me," he calls out .... He guides you down the rocky beach .... A rushing wall of water chases your footsteps across the sand .... Water drips from the hem of Jesus' garment .... "Do you see those fishermen rolling their nets?" Jesus asks, pointing to a small boat .... "I have come to see if they will help me spread the word," he hesitates, then motions for you to wait on the shore .... The fishermen look up, barely seeming to notice him .... Their expressions change quickly when Jesus calls them by name .... They stop their labors and put their nets to rest .... In a short time the fishermen and Jesus return to your resting place .... "Meet my friends Peter and his brother, Andrew,"Jesus announces .... Peter is older and scarred from a life on the sea .... Wind has eroded his face into tight wrinkles; his hands are cracked and bleeding ... He is stocky and sure of himself; he is coarse in his manner .... Andrew is much younger .... You join in with the small band of men to walk along the shoreline .... Two men are pushing their creaking vessel into the water .... Jesus walks more quickly now, "James and John, come back!" .... The men look quizzically at Jesus, but automatically return to shore ....

Jesus, his four friends, and you make plans for a journey that will last a lifetime .... The journey will be difficult .... Day soon turns into night .... Shadows of darkness invade the valley .... The four men prepare their supplies and boat .... Jesus starts a small bonfire on the shore's edge .... The sleeping sun has left in its place the chill of evening winds .... Settle yourself in the sand .... Wrap your arms tightly around yourself, shutting out the cold .... Jesus warms his hands by the fire, then takes your hands in his .... He speaks of things in your past, the people in your life, your worries and cares .... He knows you .... Your name is written in time .... Jesus does not accuse nor find fault .... He offers his love and grace .... "You have followed God's light and the way of the Gospel now lies open before you. Set your feet firmly on that path and acknowledge the living God. Walk in my light; trust in my wisdom. Commit your life to me daily so that you may believe in me with all your heart .... Turning to face you, he asks, "Will you follow in my path? Walk in my love, my dearest friend. I promise to carry you when times are hard" .... Resting now upon his haunches, he awaits your answer. (*Pause.*)

I will leave you alone with Jesus.

Prayer

Jesus, I kneel before you. Bless my ears that I may hear your voice. Bless my lips that I may respond to God's word. Bless my heart that you may dwell there by faith. I ask only that I may walk in your light. Amen.

It is time to leave .... Bid farewell to Jesus and his friends .... Walk down the rocky path .... Open your eyes and return to this room.

Discussion

Break into small groups. Maintain a quiet atmosphere, continuing to play background music if you wish. Keep the light low, asking the group to speak or respond only to the following questions:

- What did you see? What did you hear?
- What is being asked of you if you answer Jesus' call?

Closing Prayer

Let's close in silent prayer. As we pray, consider your relationship with Jesus. Looking into the past, at the present, and into your future as you would like it, how many sets of footprints could be found in the sand? (*Offer choice of possible answers.*)

- One, only the Lord's.
- One because he was carrying you.
- Two, walking side by side.
- Two, one well behind the other.

Allow time for silent meditation. Drawing to a close, form a circle, holding hands as a community. Ask for prayer petitions, then conclude with the Lord's Prayer.

Do This in Memory Of Me

Scripture: Mt 26:26–29; Mk 14:22–25; Lk 22:17–20
Feast: Holy Thursday/Lent (ABC)
Music Suggestion: "I Will Never Forget You"/*Gentle Sounds*

Although the following meditation is normally used during the season of Lent, it has been included here to augment the study and the understanding of the Eucharist, which usually occurs between the rite of acceptance and Advent.

This meditation could also be used during the preparation for the Easter Vigil and the mystagogy period.

Scripture proclaims that to share in the life of Christ, to be one with him, is to find life everlasting. Jesus invites us to share in his body and his blood, which in ancient Hebrew are symbols of both life and person. Christ offered unleavened bread, saying, "This is my body," which to the Jews meant, "This is who I am." Blood was the symbol of life. Jesus blessed the wine, raised it high, then added, "This is my blood." Thus it was and thus it still is, a new covenant in his blood.

Jesus and his followers gathered in the celebration of Passover. As was the custom they shared both food and drink, telling and retelling stories from the ancient Scripture of the Jews passing out of Egypt to the Promised Land. Our Lord chose this time of celebration to institute the Eucharist as a parting gift. Soon, you will partake of this gift, wrapping it solidly in the fibers of your faith. To see, to hear, and to be part of the celebration aid understanding. Release your imagination to travel across time to find yourself at a seder that will change the world forever ....

Meditation

Find a comfortable position .... Close your eyes .... Relax your arms and hands .... Your shoulders ....

The sun slides gently behind the rooftops to begin a time of rest .... You climb a narrow, steep stairway to join Jesus and his friends for Passover .... The aroma of roast lamb fills the stairwell .... A low murmur of voices can be heard as you near the low doorway .... Look around .... A servant boy stretches to light the oil lamps hanging from wooden pegs .... Flickering light dances with shadows .... The odor of burning oil fills your nostrils .... The disciples look up from their meal to greet you .... John stands, taking your hand .... He leads you to an empty spot at the table .... Peter, wiping food from his scruffy red beard, glances up and offers a welcoming smile .... As you begin to seat yourself upon a floor pillow, a familiar voice calls out .... Jesus quickly walks to your side .... Clasping your hand in his, he tells you, "Thank you for coming. I would have missed you greatly" ....

Jesus leads you to a place next to his at the long rough-hewn table .... He settles down on his knees, then comes to rest upon a large pillow .... The disciples recline around the table edge, occasionally partaking of the meal .... Others lean on their elbows, snatching food as it passes .... Jesus whispers in your ear, "Please pass me the basket of bread" .... Jesus takes a round piece from the basket .... It is flat and golden .... He tears off a small piece and hands it to you, "Take this and eat it, for this is my body" .... Place the bread in your mouth .... Taste the coarsely ground wheat and salt .... Jesus now offers the bread to each of his disciples .... The room is silent as each partakes of the Bread of Life .... A tear slowly moves down John's cheek, but he shares nothing of his fear for the safety of his Master .... Jesus takes his cup of wine, blesses it, making a sign of the cross above the goblet .... Turning to you, he offers the cup, "Drink from this cup, for this is my blood" .... Lowering his voice, Jesus speaks to you, "This seals a promise of love and friendship with me" .... Taste the sweetness of the grape .... Once again, he passes the cup to

each of his disciples .... Several of the men raise their hands
in silent prayer .... A shuffling of feet behind you and a
high-pitched squeak of the door hinge draw your attention ....
Judas slips through the doorway unnoticed by most of the
guests .... A shudder escapes from the lips of Jesus .... The
beginning of the end ....

Jesus breaks the cloak of silence, "I love you. My Father calls
me, but I want to be with you always. I leave you this bread
and wine to remember me for now it has become my body
and my blood" .... Each one present weighs the words of the
Lord .... Jesus leads you to a small open window .... Shutters
bang in response to a sudden wind, then hang in stillness ....
You hear only the words of your Lord .... "Remember this
moment all the days of your life; for in the time to come, this
will be your communion with me" .... Jesus takes your hands
into his .... His long thin fingers wrap gently around your
hand .... Look into his eyes .... His cheeks are wet with tears
.... Tears of anguish, tears of questioning, tears of reality stain
his face .... Feel the sweetness of his love and the sadness of
the moment .... "Do you love me?" he asks .... I will give you
time to speak with your Lord .... Listen for his voice ....

Prayer

*Jesus, I walk in your light when there is darkness. I lay
my worries at your feet. I will ask forgiveness when I
stray. In your body and blood I shall be one, united in
Christ Jesus. I love you. Amen.*

It is time for you to part .... Allow Jesus to wrap his protective
arms about you .... Hold his love tightly within your heart ....
Walk out of the room, down the stairway, and out into the
night .... Open your eyes and return to this room.

Discussion

- What did you see? What did you hear?
- To what do you most look forward about sharing
  communion for the first time at the Easter Vigil?

- Does this event bring to mind other stories from Scripture?

Although there are other stories of prophesy and symbolism, you may want to ask the group to read Exodus 12:11–17.

- How is the symbolism similar?

Closing

Depending on the time, you may wish to prepare an agape using unleavened bread and wine. Stress that this is to be a celebration of love for Jesus and for each other to signify commitment to the Lord.

Optional: Select three readers. Close with recitation of the following acclamations from Scripture*:

- You are God's work of art, created in Christ Jesus (Eph 2:10).
- All of you are one, united in Christ Jesus (Gal 3:28).
- God is love, those who live in love, live in God (1 Jn 4:16).

Response: We are God's work of art, created in Christ Jesus.

Closing Prayer

Enable us, O God, to grow in the knowledge and love of Christ so that hearts are warmed and lives are changed. In the name of the Teacher from Nazareth. Amen.

---

*"Acclamations from Sacred Scripture" (RCIA 595).

5 A Woman Caught in Adultery

Go, and Sin No More

Scripture: Jn 8:1–11

Music Suggestion: "Pardon Your People"/*Gentle Sounds*

With death but a breath away, Jesus continued to teach, heal, and forgive. Which was the greatest teaching? Which is the most amazing healing? Of all the sins forgiven, which story stays with you? (*Invite participation.*) Within the pages of Scripture, we will each find our niche in which our needs are met, our life stories are told.

Forgiveness may come in many forms during our lifetime. However, most of us feel that at sometime we have "gone over the edge." We ask ourselves, "Can he ever forgive me this time? Can I forgive myself?" These are tough questions with even tougher answers. I recall as a child committing more than a few transgressions, and then thinking that Mom or Dad would finally have their fill of forgiveness and there would be no turning back. There were punishments to be sure, but there was always forgiveness. My parents have been gone a long time; I miss knowing that there were two people on this earth who truly understood unconditional love. Our Lord washes us anew with unconditional love; we cannot earn it but we can share it.

Our Lord, knowing that the Pharisees were seeking to trick him, was confronted with a woman whose sin was punishable by death. Jesus chose not to condemn, but to forgive. Release your imaginations to travel to the temple courtyards, just beyond the Mount of Olives.

Meditation

The early light of dawn signals the birth of a new day .... The
sun raises a winking eye of light above the Temple roof ....
You have stayed behind with Jesus .... Crowds of people are
gathered to hear the teaching of your Lord .... Jesus, taking
his seat of honor among them, begins teaching once again ....
The cluster of people represents all talents, poverty, wealth,
leaders, and shepherds .... They listen with open minds and
open hearts, some still questioning, all learning .... Nearly an
hour has passed; Jesus stands stretching his arms out in
prayer .... He knows his foes are near at hand .... The
murmur of death stings the cool morning air .... Jesus walks
to your side, breaking the silence at last .... "Look ahead, my
enemies approach. The teachers of the law will not rest.
Beware, my friend, for they know nothing of God's love; they
fear his power" .... Jesus walks slowly to the center of the
courtyard .... Standing as though on cue, in the direct
center .... Small trickles of light filter through the clouds ....
A clamor of demanding voices sounds from the street
below .... Voices belonging to those who ask questions to
snare their victim .... Jesus motions for you to stand in the
shadows ....

The swarm grows larger .... Their voices loud and harsh,
accusing, scheming .... The tormented scream of a woman
startles your senses .... Scuffling feet, lighted lanterns, and the
sound of a stinging whip sing a song of subterfuge .... Jesus
stands calmly awaiting his accusers .... He places his hand
over his lips .... You must remain in silence ....

Pharisees and teachers of the law drag a screaming, filthy
woman into the yard .... Her face is young, her heart is
cold .... The woman is thrown at the feet of Jesus .... A
Pharisee, dressed in robes of honor, grabs her hair, pulling her
to her unsteady feet .... Another clutches at a piece of her
torn garment, ripping it off her shoulders .... She stands
nearly naked, bruised and bloodied .... She hides her shame
behind her hands, daring not to look upon this
judge—Jesus .... The chief Pharisee grunts her charges, "This

woman was caught in the act of adultery. The Law of Moses commands us to stone her" .... Lunging forward, nearly spitting in the face of Jesus, he bellows, "What say you, teacher?" .... His tone mocks Jesus ....

Move closer to Jesus .... Remain in the background, only he can see you .... Jesus bends down to the sandy soil beneath his feet .... He writes upon the ground .... Look over his shoulder .... What does he write? (*Pause briefly.*) Jesus straightens up, demanding of his conspirators, "If any one of you is without sin, let him be the first to throw a stone at her" .... The words of Jesus hang in the air .... Jesus once more bends to the earth and writes upon the earth .... Men struggle to see what in written upon the ground .... One by one, the men leave the Temple yard, until only Jesus and the woman remain .... Jesus stands, then asks, "Woman, where are your accusers? Has no one condemned you?" .... Clutching at her shredded clothing, she tearfully answers, "No one, sir" .... Tears of shame stain her cheeks .... Above all, she was raped, raped of all dignity .... Jesus slowly removes his outer garment .... He places it around her bare shoulders .... Taking a cloth from his pocket, he dips it into the fountain's water, then cleanses her face, her hands, and her soul .... Jesus places his hands around her face, looking directly into her eyes, "If they do not condemn you, neither do I" .... The woman falls to her knees .... Jesus lifts her to her feet, declaring, "Go now and leave your life of sin" ....

Pushcarts stream through the city's gates, farmers hawk their wares, the day has begun .... The accusers hide in shame .... And one woman, among many, will walk with shoulders back and head raised for she is forgiven ....

You and Jesus make your way down the Temple stairs .... Through the busy cobblestone streets. Jesus speaks, "Come, we shall sit for a while" .... He leads you to a rickety bench in a grove of fig trees .... Fruit hangs heavy awaiting harvest .... The sweet aroma of honeysuckle tickles your senses .... Jesus reaches forward, snagging a fragrant blossom .... He twirls it in his hand for a moment, then places it in your hands ....

Inhale the memories of springtime gone by .... The voice of Jesus breaks your reverie, "These days are hard and few in number. I am with you today so that you will forever remember the blessings of my forgiveness .... I did not condemn the woman and I shall never turn my back on you. Let us deal now with your life, and your choices .... Speak to me, how may I help you?" .... Do problems within your family weigh heavily upon you? .... Do you seek God's forgiveness?

I will allow you time to bask in the Lord's love. (*Pause.*)

Prayer

Lord, bring your peace and harmony to my family. Heal my faults that make it difficult for others to love me. Forgive my trespasses and thoughtless acts. Bless and strengthen the tie that binds our hearts in Christian love, one to another. May I rest in your peace. Amen.

It is now early afternoon and time to move on with your life .... Say good-bye to Jesus .... Take your leave .... Crossing through the trees onto the dirt road .... Open your eyes and return to this room.

Discussion

You may prefer small groups.

- What did you see? What did you hear?
- Which character in the story do you relate to?
  - The woman, ashamed, needing forgiveness
  - The condemning crowd, eager to point the finger of shame
  - Yourself, an observer only
  - Jesus, accepting and forgiving
- Are there people in your life who accept you no matter what you have done?

Closing Prayer

This may be a good time to use incense to symbolize our Lord's forgiveness—smoke rising to the heavens in offering to God. Use candlelight to spread light upon the darkness of our lives. You may wish to have several readers.

Response: I will sing your praises, O Lord God.

Leader: God is my shield; God is truth and love.

Response

Leader: Father God, you forgive my sins;
       judging with fairness and love.

Response

Leader: O Lord, I will praise you from the mountaintops
       for all your wondrous deeds.
       May all the earth hear your name
       and know your touch.

Response

Leader: I shall forever dwell in you, O Lord;
       Your forgiveness divine.
       I may stumble and fall
       but you shall not leave me.
       You have blessed me with the joys of life
       and the treasure of your eternal presence.
       Amen.*

*Based on Psalm 7:10

6 Do Not Fear

Take My Hand

Scripture: Mk 14:22–33
Feast: 19th Sunday in Ordinary Time (A)
Music Suggestion: any selection from *The Sea*
or "When You Seek Me"/*Gentle Sounds*

Jesus awaits. He calls our name from the depths of our despair. He offers his hand to steady and guide us and yet—so often, we are deaf to his call and blind to his understanding of human nature. In times of moral or physical danger, it often becomes difficult to reach out in absolute faith. For a moment, place yourself in a small fishing boat being tossed about like a cork in a bathtub. A person you have known only a short time tells you to have complete faith in him, then instructs you to step out of the boat onto a storm-tossed sea, whose depth goes well beyond the reach of sunlight. What would your answer be?

Let us spend a few moments together in prayer and meditation, united in the body of Christ, on the shore of the Sea of Galilee. The water is surrounded by hills. The wind whips around the base of the hillsides, each pass picking up speed. To this day, small craft often find themselves in danger quickly.

Meditation

Find a comfortable position .... Close your eyes .... Allow the cares of the day to drift from view .... Shrug your shoulders, releasing the tension .... Take a deep breath .... As you draw in your breath, whisper "Jesus" .... Exhale slowly .... Whisper "My Lord" ....

You are seated on the sandy shore of the Sea of Galilee ....
Water pushes onto the land, then races back into the sea,
leaving damp prints upon the shore .... Early evening
whispers its shadows across the sea .... Several small boats
prepare to cast off .... Peter moves about the deck of his boat,
storing nets and poles .... The soft winds tug at his snarled red
hair .... Peter calls out, "Ready to go!" .... Jesus climbs the
rope ladder to the edge of the deck .... Looking up he sees
you standing nearby .... He calls your name, motioning for
you to join him .... Run down to the water's edge .... Your
feet sink into the murky mire ....

Jesus, looking tired and gaunt, takes a seat on the wooden
deck, leaning against the side of the boat .... He makes room
for you beside him .... Jesus instructs the others to row to the
other side of the sea .... This will be a time away from the
milling and curious crowd .... And it will be a time of
prayer .... A time with his Father God .... Moonlight streaks
the water with a yellow haze .... Nearing the shore, a large
purple mountain rises above the water, casting a dark shadow
over the boat .... Jesus takes his leave, walking away slowly ....

You feel the gentle rolling of the waves beneath the boat ....
In the glow of the moonlight, the mountain's shadow grows
smaller .... Time passes quickly .... It is time to return for
Jesus .... The air suddenly stirs around you, whipping the sea
into frothy white foam .... Peter's hands grip the oars; his
knuckles white, he shouts, "The winds carry us farther out to
sea. We will not be able to return for Jesus!" .... You and the
disciples pull on the oars .... Blisters quickly form on your
hands .... The boat is caught in a cobweb of wind and
water .... The craft makes no headway .... A low roaring
echoes against the hills .... Darkness covers the sea .... Water
washes over the decks ....

In the direction of the distant shore, a strange figure appears
above the lake .... It moves slowly, on top of the water,
toward the boat .... James cries out, "It is surely a ghost!" ....
You peek over the railing, afraid to see and afraid not to
see .... From the shifting waters shrouded in heavy fog, you

hear .... "Do not be afraid! It is I, Jesus!" .... The ghostly
figure glides across the foamy sea .... You peer into the
fog .... It is Jesus! .... Skeptics take turns calling out, against
the wind, "Who are you?" .... "Name yourself, stranger!" ....
Jesus calls to Peter, "Come to me! Step out of the boat" ....
Peter hesitates, debating what will look the least ridiculous to
the others .... He slowly steps out of the boat, onto the cold
dark waters .... Peter immediately begins to sink .... He calls
out to the Lord, "Help me, Lord!" .... In the misty night,
Jesus reaches out to take Peter's hand, "Oh you of little faith"
.... "Why did you doubt me?" .... Jesus cradles Peter's hand
and starts walking toward the small craft .... Jesus stops,
resting upon the crest of a wave .... Clouds cover the moonlit
sky .... Jesus calls your name—not the name of James, or
even John .... He calls your name .... Can you hear him? ....
"It is time for you to step out of the boat. Walk to me, my
friend" .... I will give you time to decide if you will walk upon
the stormy sea or sit in the safety of the boat. (*Pause.*)

The waters are stilled .... The night clouded now in silence ....
Faith has shown its strength and its weakness .... You are
aware only of your heartbeat ....

Jesus, his garment soaked, settles back against the bow of the
boat .... Wrapping a blanket around your shoulders, he
speaks, "Asking you to get out of the boat was a test, you
know?" .... Jesus takes your cold hands into his, "If you could
measure your faith, is there enough to follow my path without
question?" .... Intuitively, Jesus speaks, "Spend a few
moments reflecting on those times that I have reached out for
you, only to have you move from my grasp. Where is your
faith, today, my child?" (*Pause.*)

Prayer

*Jesus, I, not unlike Peter, am afraid to test my own
faith. There are fears that come in the dark of life and
I do not place my hand in yours. Fill me with the
strength of your faith. Steady my walk with you. Bind
this community in your love, Amen.*

It is time to return to shore and say good-bye to Jesus .... Step
out of the boat onto the firmness of land .... Walk up the
sandy path .... Turn and wave one last good-bye for now ....
Open your eyes and return to this room.

Discussion

- What did you see? What did you hear?
- Is Jesus inviting you to "get out of the boat" in some area of
  your life?
- Has there been a time in your life when you felt the
  presence of the Lord?

Closing Prayer

Pray the Lord's Prayer in echo form.

The Faith That Heals

Scripture: Mk 10:46–52
Feast: 30th Sunday in Ordinary Time (B)
Music Suggestion: "When You Seek Me"/*Gentle Sounds*

Christ calls us from the darkness of our lives. He calls us to come to him and receive his light. Within the shadows that lurk ahead, in the uncertainty of faith, it is only Jesus who will heal our darkness. Only Jesus will refresh us in his love and provide peace for our journey.

A man called Bartimaeus sought out the healing touch of our Lord. Relentless in his search, Bartimaeus asked that the darkness that surrounded him be illuminated by the light of Christ. Bartimaeus' faith caused his healing. Jesus responded to the man's faith, not to his condition. Release your imaginations to travel to the city of Jericho. There we will encounter our Lord.

Meditation

Find a comfortable position .... Close your eyes .... Shut out the sounds and cares of the day .... Allow Jesus to cover you with calm, starting with your mind .... Your shoulders .... Your arms fall limp .... Take a deep breath .... Exhale .... Whisper "Jesus" ....

You stand outside the gates of the city of Jericho .... Clouds of dust settle heavily upon the air .... Citizens push empty carts to the marketplace .... Others bring wagons loaded with lambs and chickens .... For Sale signs hang limply on the side of wooden stalls .... Jesus picks several green apples from a street vendor. Handing one to you, he then passes the apples to Peter ....

7. The Faith That Heals

Narrow cobblestone streets lead into the city .... Tall steeples reach toward the heavens .... Jesus leads, motioning for you to hurry along .... He takes the right road .... Large buildings fill the horizon .... A young man sits among his tattered belongings begging for food .... He is thin and frail .... Clearly, the man and a bath have never met .... His skeletal frame is covered in rags .... You turn to tell Jesus of this pitiful sight, only to find that he has nearly been swallowed by the gathering crowd .... The man calls out, "What is going on?" .... You answer, "Jesus of Nazareth is here" .... The blind man raises his voice, "Jesus, Son of David, have mercy on me!" .... Jesus turns sharply, asking Peter, "Who is that man?" .... A woman from the city answers coldly, "It is only Bartimaeus, the town beggar" .... Disgust lingers in the air .... "Don't give him the time of day," shouts another .... The crowd surges forward, separating you from Jesus ....

A nearby soldier warns Bartimaeus to quiet down .... The blind man calls out louder, "Son of David, have mercy on me!" .... Jesus turns toward you, then signals for you to bring Bartimaeus to his side .... Whisper in Bartimaeus' ear .... He jumps up quickly, spilling his small basket of coins .... Take his hand; it is thin and fragile, his skin nearly transparent .... His walk is unsteady, shaking with excitement .... Lead him to Jesus ....

Jesus, always compassionate, takes Bartimaeus' soiled, scaly hand in his, "What do you want from me, my son?" .... The man's eyes are clouded with darkness .... He begs Jesus, "Grant that I may see the world with these eyes" .... Jesus looks squarely into the sightless eyes, then announces, "I am the light of the world!" .... Bending down, he mixes saliva and dirt in his hand and makes a mud paste .... He smears the mud over Bartimaeus' eyes .... Bartimaeus sits encased in darkness .... Jesus walks away, seeking the cleansing waters of a fountain .... Jesus calls out, "Bring the man to me. He shall wash the mud from his eyes" .... Bartimaeus places his hand upon your shoulder .... You lead him to the bubbling fountain .... Pour the cool waters into his waiting hands .... Dip your hands into the water .... Cleanse the eyes of the dark-skinned man .... He shudders with sudden cold .... When the last spot of mud is washed clean, Bartimaeus opens his eyes ....

The veil of blindness that once covered the man's eyes has disappeared .... In contrast, his brown eyes reflect the light of day .... "I can see!" he shouts in joy .... Jesus chuckles to himself .... The crowd buzzes with excitement, enveloping the man they shunned moments before ....

Jesus quickly leaves the crowd behind, leading you to the shelter of a lone olive tree .... You take a seat on a large boulder .... Jesus rests his back against the tree .... "I was sent into this world to make people see not only with their eyes but also with their hearts" .... "But why Bartimaeus?" you question .... Jesus smiles, "He just would not give up. In all of his darkness, with eyes that saw nothing, he knew that I was the Son of God. He saw the light that shines within .... God is light. In him there is no darkness. Bartimaeus has the gift of faith" .... The gentle breath of spring tugs at his hair, lashing loose strands across his face.... Jesus takes one hand and pulls his hair into a knot at the back of his head .... He continues, "Many are blind to the love and forgiveness of God .... Some may be blind to the goodness in others .... More than a few hide in the darkness of life, afraid to call out to me with faith, for fear that I may not answer" .... Jesus raises to one knee, taking your hand in his, "My friend, do you believe in me and the power of faith? Come to me in faith, child" ....

I will give to you time to answer your Lord. Jesus comes to us even when we are blinded by life. (*Pause.*)

Prayer

Jesus, forgive me for those times that I have failed to see the hand of God in my life. May I see more clearly. Allow my faith to reside in my heart, silently stalking doubts and insecurities. May your presence abound. My faith is aglow with your light. Amen.

A Light in the Midst Of Darkness

Scripture: Mt 5:14–16
Music Suggestion: "Only a Shadow"/*Gentle Sounds*

Meditation

Find a comfortable position .... Close your eyes .... Relax your body .... Allow your mind to shut out the sounds and cares of the day .... Breathe in .... Breathe out .... Take a deep breath in .... Breathe out .... Concentrate on your breathing .... The world lies in stillness .... You bask in the love of your Lord, Jesus. (*Pause.*)

Though your eyes remain closed, you are aware of a strong light in the room .... The image of Jesus sits nearby .... His hand is outstretched .... In the center of his palm, a ball of white light radiates his love, his forgiveness, his healing .... The shroud of darkness is lifted .... The figure of Jesus disappears from view .... Only light lingers, chasing shadows from your life ....

You and the light of Jesus are all that remain in the room ....

Breathe in the light of Christ .... Breathe the light of Jesus into your whole being .... As you exhale, the light of Christ spreads throughout the room .... The light shines from within, enveloping your body and soul ....

The words of Jesus echo in your mind ....

> *You are now the light of the world.*
> *A city upon a hill cannot be hidden.*
> *You do not light a lamp and hide it beneath a bowl.*
> *No, it is placed on its stand, to give light to all.*
>
> *In the same way, my light now shines in you.*
> *Allow the world to see by my light,*
> *In you, they shall see me ....*

Be aware of only your heartbeat .... Breathe in the light of Christ .... Exhale his love .... His healing .... His forgiveness ....

As a symbol of the light of Christ, we ask that each of you come forward with your taper, one at a time, to light it from the community candle.

Allow a few minutes for silent reflection in this atmosphere.

Leader: May the light of Christ travel with you to illuminate and enlighten your journey of faith.

Close with the Lord's Prayer.

Make Ready Your Heart

Scripture: Mt 3:1–12; Mk 1:1–8; Mk 13:33–37
Feast: 1st or 2nd Sunday of Advent (ABC)
Music Suggestion: any selection from *The Sea*
    or "When You Seek Me"/*Gentle Sounds*

Early Christians believed that the end of the world was imminent and that Jesus would return to conquer the world. Because the world was going to end at any moment, the disciples felt no need to write down the events of Jesus' life, they just passed the stories on verbally from person to person. It took thirty-five or more years before the Gospel of Mark was even written. This can be referred to as "taking your time." Jesus, more than likely, had other plans.

Perhaps there is a strong message in this for us today. Most of us believe that we have plenty of time to "straighten out " our lives. But do we? John the Baptist didn't think so, and he sent a warning to the people of Israel that it was indeed time to clean up their act. The Scriptures for the First Sunday of Advent call us to be alert. Our Lord God sent forth this man called John the Baptist to remind us to "prepare the way of the Lord."

This is also our time to prepare our hearts for Jesus—to put away those things that would make Jesus feel unwelcome. John had yet another mission: He would baptize Jesus in the River Jordan. The power of the Holy Spirit would settle upon our Lord, wrapping him in God's love and providing strength to fulfill his mission in this life. Let us release our imaginations to travel to the shore of the Jordan River. Perhaps we will actually be able to see John the Baptist and hear his message on our journey.

Meditation

Find a comfortable position .... Close your eyes .... Shut out the sights and sounds of the day .... Take a deep breath .... Let it out slowly .... Whisper "Jesus" ....

You feel the warm autumn sun on your face .... You are walking down a crooked road .... Grains of sand sweep across your feet as your walk .... Stop and remove your shoes, sending sand and grit flying upon the breeze .... In the distance a grove of trees stands at attention along the shore of the Jordan River .... Tree limbs dance on the wind .... Inviting you to enjoy their shade .... Move quickly now to stand beneath the protective arms of the trees .... Settle down onto the sand, leaning against the bent olive tree .... Nearby the waters of the Jordan River splash against the shore .... A large crowd is gathered at the riverside .... Near the water's edge, you see the man called John the Baptist .... He is dressed in the skins of animals, his hair hangs in long dreadlocks .... He speaks firmly, urging the crowd to join him in the washing waves of the river ....

His voice is carried upon the wind, "Prepare the way for the coming of God!" .... John stands ragged, a thick leather belt around his waist. He motions wildly with his arms .... You study this man .... Would you choose him for a friend? .... John turns, looking directly at you, then he motions for you to join him .... "What does he want of me?" you ask yourself .... There is a gentle touch on your shoulder .... Jesus has joined you in the shade of a myrtle tree .... He smiles and calls you by name .... His face grows serious, "I would like you to meet John. He is sent by my Father to prepare the hearts of the people for my coming .... The people gathered here have never heard of me .... John knows of my coming but not yet of my presence. None have been baptized to a new life in God" .... Jesus begins to pace back and forth, pushing the hair from his eyes .... His voice is low and resonant, "If God

42

were to ask you to tell the others about me, what would you
tell them?" .... Take a few minutes to answer Jesus. (*Pause.*)

Feeling the weight of Jesus' words, you slowly make your way
down the hillside toward John .... This is unfamiliar
ground .... You hesitate .... Jesus remains beneath the tree,
nodding encouragement ....

The people are churning about in the waters, questioning the
strange-looking man, probably without understanding the task
before him .... "Are you the promised one?"sings out a
member of the crowd .... John walks toward you, reaching
out to take your hand in his .... John's eyes soften .... His
gaze becomes intent but clearly questioning your presence ....
At long last he speaks, "The Lord is near. He has sent you.
Come, my friend, there is much to do to prepare for the
coming of God" .... John wraps his arm about your shoulders,
walking toward the shore .... He leans close, whispering,
"Begin today by looking into your own heart. Sweep away all
the needless duties and obligations that crowd your world" ....

John settles down on the riverbank .... You take a seat upon a
large rock, splintered by time .... In the space of silence you
recall those hurts and anger that you have hidden from sight.
(*Pause briefly.*) Reflect upon the times you may have
forgotten to make someone else's road easier. (*Pause briefly.*)
These things may be swept away .... Slowly, you rise,
returning to where Jesus stands waiting for you ....

Jesus greets you with open arms .... I will leave you alone with
Jesus to eliminate the cobwebs of time and anguish .... Jesus
knows your heart. (*Pause until the group becomes restless.*)

Prayer

*Jesus, I have stockpiled so much garbage in my life.
Help me to sort through the unnecessary tasks and
duties. With your grace I shall prepare my own heart
for your coming. Do not let the shadows of my life
darken the path to everlasting life. May your light
shine through my eyes and the works of my hands.
Amen.*

Discussion

Form small groups for sharing. Suggest that each group contemplate the following questions and be prepared to share the consensus of their answers.

- Has there been a John the Baptist in your life (someone who led you to God)?
- If God asked you to tell the people of your community about Jesus, what could you tell them?
- How will you use this Advent season to prepare for Jesus' coming?

Prayer Time

Dim the lights or use candlelight. Continue to play background music.

Reflection: Reflect quietly on your lives.

Pause after each question for reflection time.

- Call to mind the rough edges that need to be sanded down.
- Do you need to reach out to someone, but you don't know how?
- Is there a situation at home or in the workplace that you need insight into?
- Reflect on those close to you who may need to have the guiding hand of Jesus.

Response: Lord, hear our prayers.

Leader: We gather together to ask for your healing touch on people around the world.

Response

Leader: For all those who are suffering from an addiction of any kind, we pray to the Lord.

Response

Leader: For those who are lost and cannot find their way home to Jesus, we pray to the Lord.

Response

Leader: For our own personal needs, we pray to the Lord.

Allow a few minutes for them to volunteer prayer petitions.

Response

Leader: We pray that each of us may find our own path to the Lord, following it all the days of our lives.

Response

Close by holding hands in a circle and saying the Lord's Prayer.

A Morning with Mary

Scripture: Mt 1:18–25; Lk 1:26–38
Feast: 4th Sunday of Advent (AB)
Music Suggestion: any selection from *Dream Journey*
      or "Hail, Mary, Gentle Woman"/*Gentle Sounds*

When God chose the angel Gabriel to deliver his message to
Mary, Gabriel really had his work cut out for him. First of all,
the message was going to a young teenage girl. Most of us
would consider the message rather earth-shattering; it
probably turned her world upside-down. Gabriel also had to
consider that the "plan" was in everyone's best interest. As
parents, most of us would argue that point.

God knew his subject well. Mary, a model of faith for the
generations to come, had unqualified faith, and she loved God.
It is very probable that she didn't understand what was
happening to her or why, or where her own journey would
take her. But with steadfast love of God, she sent a message
proclaiming that she would carry the Son of God into the
world and all the worlds to come.

Let us spend a few moments with Mary on the morning of
Gabriel's arrival. Gabriel has just awakened Mary from a
sound sleep.

Meditation

Find a comfortable position .... Close your eyes .... Shut away
the sounds and cares of the day .... Your arms fall limp ....
Take a deep breath .... Let it out slowly .... Inhale one more
time, holding it for a few seconds .... Relax .... Whisper
"Jesus" ....

It is very early morning .... The sun peaks over the hills of
Galilee .... Birds awaken to the new day .... You are curled up
in your bed, covered with tattered quilt .... Mary's cot is
opposite yours .... Slowly and quietly you turn in your
covers .... You look over at Mary .... Long dark hair
surrounds her young innocent face .... Mary is sitting bolt
upright, startled out of a sound sleep .... There is a bright light
in the room .... An angel stands at the foot of Mary's wobbly
bed .... Thoughts of alarm enter your mind, only to be
dispelled by the aura of calm and peace .... Mary grasps her
ragged blanket about her, motioning for you to sit beside
her .... She trembles beneath the covers .... The angel speaks,
"Good morning, Mary," then slowly turns to greet you also ....
The angel calls you by name .... "Do not be afraid, I have not
come to harm you" .... Can you hear the angel's voice? ....
Mary places a protective arm about your shoulders and smiles
at the angel .... "My name is Gabriel," the angel announces...

"Do not be afraid, Mary, God has sent me to tell you that a
male child is about to be born .... At his birth he is to be called
Jesus, a name that means, 'Yahweh saves' .... Mary's eyes
spell confusion, but her spirit is sincere .... The angel
continues, "God asks if you are willing to be this child's
mother. Your son will be called the Son of God .... But, if for
any reason, you ..."".... His words trail off in midair .... Mary
quickly scoots to the edge of her bed, falling upon her knees in
prayer .... The beautiful young woman reaches out her hand,
gesturing for you to join her in prayer .... The floor beneath
you grows cold and hard .... Mary speaks, at long last,
"Whatever God asks of me, I will do. I do not understand, but I
will trust in God .... I will be the mother of this child" ....

The angel smiles, disappearing as quickly as he appeared ....
Mary reaches out to you once again, pulling you next to
her .... She rises to sit on her bed, her back resting against the
wall .... Mary wraps your cold legs in her well-worn
blanket .... Study her face closely .... "I know there are
questions to be answered and I do not know the answers.
There are times in our lives when we must put our whole trust
in God. We cannot question or make deals" ....

47

Take this time to speak to Mary .... Mary always hears our prayers. Through her great faith she will lead you to trust God's wisdom for your life .... The mother of God will hear your prayers. (*Pause.*)

Prayer

Dearest Mary, I fall on bended knee before you. All honor is yours as the mother of God. Help me to be steadfast in my own faith, looking for God's plans for my life, instead of my own. Guide me on my walk with your Son, the Lord. Let me not stumble and lose my way. Amen.

It is time to leave Mary's side .... Mary wraps her arms about you, holding you close .... Say good-bye .... Turn and leave the room, walking out into the early morning mist .... Open your eyes and return to this room.

Discussion

Form small groups of both men and women. Ask the women to reflect and answer the following questions.

- Put yourself in Mary's position. You are very young, unmarried, and the man you are engaged to is thinking of leaving you. Would your faith in God enter into your decision?

- Have you had a similar experience that required full faith in God?

Prayer Time

Light a large candle. Place a rose beside the candle. Play the background music. Provide pencils and papers. Gift wrap a small box, then cut a slit in top. If appropriate, insert the pink candle in the Advent wreath and light it. Select someone to read: Mark 13:33–37

Reflection: The story of Mary and Joseph is one of absolute trust in God. Mary, not much more than a child, had the wisdom and faith to say yes to God. God is waiting for our

answer. Take a moment to reflect upon an area in your life
where you need to reach out in faith and say yes to God.

*After writing, ask that they fold the paper several times,
writing their name on the outside of the folded paper.
Invite everyone to come forward and place the paper in the
sealed gift box. The box can remain in the room to be
opened during the last retreat, when you ask them to
reflect on what they wrote several months before and to
assess how far they have come.*

Leader: Mary, through your example, we have grown to
understand the meaning of faith. We come before you
with our dreams, hopes, problems, and prayers.
Blessed is the "fruit of thy womb, Jesus."
We open our hearts and lives to the love of God.
Through the grace of your Son, Jesus, may we
become bonded in God's love. Amen.

Invite individual prayers of petition.

Response: Lord of wonder, Lord of light, hear our prayers.

In the Still of the Night

Scripture: Lk 2:1–16
Feast: Christmas (ABC)
Music Suggestion: "When You See Me"/*Gentle Sounds*
  or "Some Children See Him"/*December*

It came to pass, in the days of Caesar Augustus, the Roman
ruler, that a law was passed that everyone within his reign
should be counted. Farmers, carpenters, weavers, elders, rich,
and poor traveled to the town where they were born and
registered their families in a book of census. While Joseph and
Mary were in Bethlehem, the time came for the birth of
Mary's child. Let us release our imaginations to walk with
Mary and Joseph in the joy of
the season.

Meditation

Find a comfortable position .... Become very still .... Close
your eyes .... Allow the sounds and cares of the day to drift
into nothingness .... Let your body relax .... Travel to the days
so long ago .... Take a deep breath .... Whisper "Jesus" ....
Feel the quiet cover like a warm blanket on a cold winter's
day ....

It is just before sunset .... The day is about to be clouded by
the hand of darkness .... You have covered many miles
today .... Your legs grow weary .... The flickering lights of
Bethlehem lie ahead .... The air is cold and filled with the
smoke of weary travelers' campfires ....

Joseph, the carpenter, looking younger than you expected,
walks beside you, his dark hair falling to his shoulders ....
Joseph turns in your direction, "The city will be very crowded.

11. In the Still of the Night

I pray there will be a room for us" .... Mary, large with child, sits upon the donkey's back, rocking back and forth with the rhythm of his gait .... Her cheeks are blushed with the cold; her eyes are nearly closed .... She is but a child .... Nearing the city gates, Joseph hands you the reins as he runs off to find shelter .... You lead the beast through the gates .... The strain of travel shows on the faces and nerves of all who have gathered here .... You almost lose your grip on the donkey's reins as you are shoved to the ground .... Mary shudders, then lets out a sigh ....

At last, Joseph returns .... His steps are heavy .... He shakes his head no .... Mary leans over, whispering in Joseph's ear .... Joseph sets out quickly .... Mary lets out a deep sigh and reaches out to grasp your hand, "The child is coming soon!" .... Your heart skips a beat .... You must find shelter .... Once more, Joseph returns without finding shelter .... Determined to help, you scurry off toward the back door of a large inn .... You knock on the door, begging for a small space of safety and warmth .... At long last, the innkeeper reluctantly motions down the road .... He says you will find a cave there .... It shelters animals from the weather, but it will serve as the birthing place for the King of Kings ....

Joseph gently lifts the small, swollen figure of Mary down from the bony back of the donkey .... He speaks firmly, motioning toward the stacks of hay, "Friend, go ahead and make a bed for Mary" .... Quickly you gather the hay into a pile, smoothing it out with your hands .... Taking off the blanket that covers your shoulders, you spread it out on top of the bed .... The sweet smell of hay fills your nostrils .... A small lamb nestles against his mother for warmth .... From within the darkness of the cave, a cow's mournful lowing sounds a welcome .... God's creatures sense the mystery .... Joseph carries Mary to the makeshift bed you have prepared for her ....

Leave Mary and Joseph now; for this is their time .... This is God's time .... In the corner of the cave, you lie back against the prickly hay .... You begin to pray .... The presence of

God surrounds you .... God is here. (*Pause.*) Minutes dissolve into hours .... At last, in the still of the night, a baby's soft cry signals new life .... A cry that will someday bring the world to its knees .... Joseph speaks softly, "The child is a boy. His name shall be Jesus" .... Joseph leads you to Mary's resting place .... Mary smiles weakly as you enter .... The baby rests in her arms .... Joseph strokes the child's head .... Look at Jesus .... He is so perfect, so small .... A tear of wonder, a tear of joy falls gently upon your cheek .... Kneel in his presence .... The hopes and fears of all the years are met in this child tonight .... Give thanks to God for the gift of life .... life everlasting ....

Mary rises on one elbow, inviting you to come closer .... She holds out her newborn son for you to hold .... "Would you like to hold Jesus," she asks .... Mary places the sleeping child in your arms .... Feel the warmth of life .... Feel the miracle of this birth. (*Pause.*) Time stands still .... The Savior is born. (*Pause.*)

Prayer

Jesus, in the stillness of this night I have held you in my arms. I am blessed with your presence. God's kingdom shall reign. Amen.

If you listen very closely, you will hear all the angels in heaven singing songs of praise to God .... "Glory to God in the highest and peace on earth to people of goodwill."

It is now early morning .... Crowds gather outside the cave .... Shepherds from nearby fields offer praise to God .... The shepherds tell of an angel who appeared in fields where they lay, bringing news of great joy, "In the city of Bethlehem, a Savior has been born. The Savior is Christ the Lord" ....

It is time to leave this night of wonder .... Bend low to kiss the cheek of the babe .... In times to come, you will wipe away his tears and the blood from his cheek .... Press your lips against his delicate hand .... Rise, and walk through the entrance of the cave .... Into the misty dawn of time .... Open your eyes and return to this room.

Discussion

- What did you see? What did you hear?
- What is your favorite part of the Christmas story?

Following His Star

Scripture: Mt 2:1–12
Feast: Epiphany (ABC)
Music Suggestion: any selection from *Dream Journey*
 or "Some Children See Him"/*December*

During the time of Jesus, people believed a new star appeared in the sky each time a child was born. On such a night, a group of Wise Men, meaning educated and knowledgeable people, spotted an extremely bright star in the sky. They understood this to mean that someone very important had been born. Remembering Scriptures of old, they felt surely the Messiah had been born. These men were from countries to the east of Bethlehem; they were not Jews. Perhaps Matthew was trying to tell us that Jesus was born for everyone, not *just* for the Jewish nation.

Let us release our imaginations, joining the Wise Men in their search for the infant born in a simple stable, our Lord of Lords, Jesus Christ.

Meditation

Find a comfortable position …. Close your eyes …. Roll your shoulder back and forth, releasing the tensions of the day …. Let stillness settle within you …. Take a deep breath …. Let it out slowly …. Whisper "Jesus" ….

With eyes that see from within, look into the ancient past …. You are standing near the gates of the city of Jerusalem …. It is evening …. Glowing lanterns send shimmers of light to bid welcome to the night …. People scurry about loading carts with treasures, hurrying to their homes …. A small group of men move in the distance …. They point excitedly to the sky .... The men stop, just outside the gate, sending one man ahead .... A tall, dark-skinned man, dressed in a flowing red cloak, speaks to you, "Where is the King of the Jews? We have followed his star from the east and have come to worship him" .... Having heard this, you offer to take the men to the cave, knowing there is nothing to fear .... The men, bearing dust and fatigue from their journey, leave their pack animals and three wrapped packages with you .... You settle down on your haunches to wait ....

Clusters of armed soldiers question nearby merchants on the location of the newborn baby .... A soldier, his sword gleaming, mounts the nearest horse, galloping toward King Herod's castle .... A shudder moves through you in the cold of the evening .... The three men from the East return, rested and fed .... They pack their belongings onto the backs of the donkeys .... A trumpet sounds in the background, signaling the appearance of the king .... Not leaving a stone unturned, Herod's armies search for the King of the Jews .... You hurry the Wise Men along on their quest ....

As night settles its cloak of darkness across the land, you and the Wise Men embark .... The night sky is darkened except for the brilliant light from the star .... It appears to travel just ahead of the journeyers .... Its brilliance casts the shadow of a path across the night .... The men all talk at once, pointing toward the sky .... "What will you bring the new king?" a voice calls out in the night air .... "I have brought a gift of rare perfume" answers another .... The man dressed in a cape of fur looks your way, saying nothing .... Your hands quickly scan your pockets .... Surely, you must not come before the new king with empty pockets ....

After hours of travel, you reach Bethlehem .... The star fairly gleams with light, removing the shroud of darkness from cobblestone streets and rows of little houses .... The only sound is that of the donkeys' hooves and the quiet, almost reverent, shuffling of footsteps .... The star stops .... A path of light falls now upon a small cave hidden in the shadows .... The glow of a lantern flickers from within .... A crude wooden

door covers the entrance to the stable .... Sheep and cows lie
side by side upon the cold earth near the entrance .... The
three men stop and dismount, removing three gifts from the
packs .... Joseph stands in the doorway. He greets you
warmly, offering his calloused hand .... Joseph waves for the
men to come inside and see his son ....

Mary sits upon a bed of straw, rocking back and forth .... She
holds her son in her arms .... At the sound of your voice, the
baby turns his head toward you, as though he knows you ....
A knowledge that goes beyond his age .... Your heart
pounds .... This is your Lord .... This is your Savior .... You
fall on bended knee, giving thanks to God for lighting the path
to Jesus .... Once again, you search your empty pockets ....

The Wise Men kneel at the foot of the manger, giving thanks
to God for the wonder of this night .... The gift of gold shines
in the light of a nearby lantern .... The gifts of frankincense
and myrrh are yet to be opened .... Mary places her hand on
yours, "I think he knows you," she says, nodding toward the
child ....

I will leave you alone for a moment .... You look more closely
at the infant .... These are not the blue eyes of an ordinary
child. The past and the future of life are cast in his gaze ....
Take this time to speak to the infant Jesus .... He will know
the gift that you place in offering .... There is no monetary
value; it is more precious than gold .... Reflect upon this ....
Perhaps your gift will be merely a promise that will stay within
your heart ....

Prayer

*Jesus, I, like Herod, at times find it easier to offer
anything but myself to God. In my past, I have
followed the wrong star to a place hidden in darkness.
Light my path clearly. Share my burdens. I give you
my love and a promise wrapped in faith. Amen.*

The sun calls out to a new day .... The Wise Men have begun
their journey back to their homelands .... It is time now for
you to leave .... Walk out the splintered wooden door of the

stable .... A rooster crows in the distance, a welcome to the sun .... Walk down the cobblestone streets .... Open your eyes and return to this room.

Discussion

In small groups discuss the answers to the following questions:

- What did you see? What did you hear?
- The Three Wise Men gave the best gifts they could give to the child Jesus. If you had the ability to be present at his birth today what gift would you offer?

Allow the group to look through wallets, pockets, or purses for a symbolic gift. Share the symbol of the gift and why it was chosen.

Closing Prayers

Dim the room, lighting one large candle. (Optional: votive candles placed in 5-ounce cups.) Play background music. They will light individual candles from the large candle, signifying the light of Christ.

Leader: On this day we come together to remember the Wise Men of long ago. We, too, must look to the heavens and follow the path of your star.

Please come forward to light your candle from the flame of this community candle. This light offers us a visible sign of the light of your presence among us. Please repeat this response as you light your candle:

Response: You are with us, Lord.

Leader: May your light shine within us.

Response

Leader: Light the path on our journey of faith.

Response

Leader: May we see your light in others.

Response

Leader: We offer you our gift of love,
our prayers of hope and faith
held dearly within our hearts.

Response

Close with the Lord's Prayer.

A Voice over the Water

Scripture: Mt 3:11-17; Mk 1:7-11; Lk 3:15-16,21-22
Feast: Baptism of the Lord (ABC)
Music Suggestion: "Sea of Change"/*Ceremony*
     or "By Name I Have Called You"/*Gentle Sounds*

Would you agree that God provides a John the Baptist, or
perhaps several if we are stubborn, in our own lives? Is there
someone who has been a John the Baptist in your life,
preparing you to meet the Lord?

Jesus, the Son of God and sinless, chose to be baptized by
John along with hundreds of simple desert people. Within the
pages of Scripture, Isaiah proclaimed the birth of Christ, the
life story of Jesus, our Lord. Jesus knew that it was
proclaimed that God would send a messenger to prepare for
his coming. Jesus stood on a hillside listening to the words of
John. Knowing that his cousin, John, was sent by the Father,
Jesus walked into the cool waters of the Jordan River to be
baptized. Let's release our imaginations to join Jesus near the
shores of the Jordan River.

Meditation

Find a comfortable position .... Close your eyes .... Allow
your body to grow limp and relaxed .... Shut out the sounds
and problems of the day .... Imagine the sound of water
cascading down a mountain creek, and the life it gives .... It is
calm; it is peaceful .... The sweet smell of a recent rain fills
your nostrils .... The sun warms the back of your neck and
your shoulders ....

The dark green waters of the Jordan River wash against the
parched shore .... The valley is brown and barren with the

exception of a few small trees dotting the landscape .... You
walk toward the river .... Your feet slip and slide out of control
on the loose rocks .... There are footsteps not far behind
you .... "May I walk with you?" a soft voice calls out .... You
turn .... It is Jesus! .... Jesus calls your name, smiling
warmly .... "Come, let me steady you, so you don't slip on the
path" .... Place your hand on his arm .... His skin is bronzed
from days in the desert sun ....

You are nearly at the bottom of the hillside when Jesus points
to a large crowd gathered on the shore .... With a wide
expanse of his arms, he gestures, "All of these people have
come to be baptized by my cousin John" .... Jesus steps up
his pace .... You are almost running to keep up with him ....
Clouds of sand billow over your feet as your stride
lengthens .... John stands amidst the swirling waters .... A belt
of rope clings to his garments made of animal skins .... His
hair hangs in long twisted knots .... People wade out into the
waiting waters of the river .... John bends low, his hands
cupped, dipping into the water, then slowly, gently, immersing
them in the life-giving waters .... A young, slim woman stands
before John, her long hair falling into wet ringlets .... Jesus,
knowing your questions, answers, "These people ask for
baptism, asking that the Spirit of God will strengthen their
walk with the Messiah .... They prepare for my coming" ....
Questions flood your mind ....

Jesus walks quickly into the water, inviting you to join him,
"John shall baptize you, with your permission, and then
me" .... Still grasping Jesus' arm, you step into the cool water
of the Jordan .... Jagged rocks cut into your bare feet ....
Long fingers of marsh grass wrap about your legs .... The
river waters, cold beyond the first swim of summer, pound
relentlessly against the shore, knocking you off balance ....
Jesus reaches forward, steadying your steps .... The water is
so cold that your legs burn, and then are numb .... John the
Baptist glances up, and smiles, calling out your name .... He
places large, rough hands on your shoulders .... "I am
baptizing you with this water, but someone is coming who is
greater than I. I am not worthy of tying his sandals. He will

60

baptize you with the Holy Spirit" .... Without looking up, John once again dips his hands into the frigid water, then slowly pours the water over your head .... John lowers you into the river .... Sand and rocks ooze through your toes .... The instant chill passes .... New life fills your body .... You stand now, rocking unsteadily in the waves ....

Water spills slowly down your face .... Lick your lips .... Taste the water .... Reach into the river, splash your face once again .... Jesus smiles, then takes his place before John ....

Jesus bows his head .... Recognition fills John's eyes, a tear of joy forms on his cheek .... "Jesus, you should baptize me" .... Jesus shakes his head no, then whispers to John .... Jesus raises his hands in prayer as John begins to spill the river waters over the head of the Son of Man ....

Jesus raises his hands to the heavens, his cloak heavy with water .... The clouds lying in wait begin to separate .... A large white dove appears above Jesus' head .... Listen to the silence .... In the quiet of the moment, you hear the gentle brush of angels' wings signaling the voice of God. (*Pause briefly.*) A deep voice from far beyond the white clouds announces, "This is my Son. He is my beloved" .... Instantly, your breath catches in the back of your throat; your skin is cold and clammy with fear .... The murmuring crowd gasps in wonder and fear .... Shepherds, farmers, and vineyard workers alike, fall on their knees in reverence to God ....

Jesus returns to your side .... Water drips from his beard .... His eyes glisten with hope .... Clouds suddenly shadow his face then rush off with the speed of the wind .... Days of foreboding lie in the future .... Today, Father God has spoken, and all is right with the world .... You and Jesus walk hand-in-hand to shore .... Jesus stops near broken pilings .... He speaks quietly, "My friend, God has called you by name .... The Holy Spirit of God rests within your heart" .... The pounding of your heart echoes in your ears .... Jesus pulls off his wet outer garment, resting his back against a boulder that has broken free from the earth .... The sun warms your back with the rays of the day .... "Remember, that God has

chosen you to carry the message of the kingdom of God" ....
You struggle against the burden of his words .... Taking your
hand in his, he leans closer, "I will show you the way. New
strengths will emerge. Will you share your life with me?" ....

Take this time to be with Jesus .... Listen to his words with
your heart. (*Pause.*)

Prayer

*Jesus, I fall before you, weak and frail against the
strife of life. Strengthen me with your Holy Spirit.
Enable my heart to reflect your light to others. Amen.*

It is time to leave .... Place your hand upon his .... Feel the
smoothness of his skin, the gentleness of his touch .... Tell
Jesus good-bye for now .... Turn and walk up the hillside ....
Open your eyes and return to this room.

Discussion

- What did you see? What did you hear?
- What new strength would you like to see emerge as a gift of
  the Holy Spirit?
- How can you follow the path of Jesus this coming week?

Prayer Service

*Before the session prepare a table with two bowls of water
(placing one on either end of the table), a white garment, a
a baptismal candle, and a large candle. Prior to the prayer
service, remind the group of the symbolism of the objects.
Dim the lights. Light the large candle.*

Response: I do, Lord.

Leader: We are brothers and sisters in God's family. Let us
refresh ourselves in the promise of baptism to live as
Jesus did.

Response

A Time for Change

Scripture: Jn 2:13–25
Feast: 3rd Sunday of Lent (B)
Music Suggestion: any selection from *Dream Journey*
or "I Will Never Forget You"/ *Gentle Sounds*

Have you personally observed an incident recently that demonstrated a lack of justice? Was it in your workplace? neighborhood? church? (*Allow time for a brief explanation of the incident.*) Did observing this breach of social justice make you want to do something about it or did it make you feel helpless to change the situation? Can anger be constructive? (*Absolutely.*) What would it take to push you into action? I believe that Jesus would tell us, "Don't talk the talk if you can't walk the walk." In other words, "Get out of your chair, stop grumbling about injustice, and do something about it—no matter how small the act may be."

Scriptures show Jesus was involved in real life with all of its anguish and heartbreak. It was not enough for Jesus to "talk the talk," he took positive action. In today's society, what would trigger his anger and concern?

Is it ever enough to just feel incensed? Probably not. In order to walk his walk, we may need to see how Jesus handled social injustice. Our imaginative journey will take us to a place of worship, the Temple, a place to give honor to God.

In the custom of the day, Jews offered sacrifices to God in the Temple. They believed they should offer only the healthiest animals as a sacrifice as God deserved only the best. At times the priests and cagey merchants used this belief to cheat the poor. Unscrupulous people have roamed the earth since time began.

The victims of their scams were usually the poor who were unable to protect themselves. A common scenario was the poor Jewish shepherd who would pick out his best sheep to take to the Temple to serve as an offering to God. When he arrived at the Temple, a priest would inspect the animal and state that it was "unfit for sacrifice." The shepherd then had the choice of making the long trip home for another animal or following the priest's suggestion of purchasing a "guaranteed perfect" animal from the merchant just beyond the Temple gates. However, the cost was very high. The priest who rejected the first animal would receive a cut from the merchant for sending the shepherd to his stall.

Moneychangers also set up tables in the area. The pilgrims had to pay a Temple tax with Jewish currency. They could not use Roman coins, because they were engraved with the image of the emperor, whom the Romans worshiped as a god. The moneychangers made huge profits by exchanging the Roman coins for less than they were really worth. They would then bribe the priest of the Temple to allow them to do business. The poor honest people wishing to pay homage to their God were victimized. Have things changed much since the days of Christ? Would this make you angry?

Let's release our imaginations to travel with Jesus into the city of Jerusalem. We shall visit the Temple and see what drives Jesus to anger.

Meditation

Find a comfortable spot .... Let you arms fall at rest .... Close your eyes .... Take a deep breath .... Let it out slowly .... Whisper "Jesus" .... Relax

It is a warm spring day .... Soft winds blow the desert sands into rising spirals of debris .... As Passover nears, the city square is filled with merchants and visitors .... Jesus takes a determined stride down the well-traveled road .... "Where are we going?" you ask .... "To the Temple, it is time to make our sacrifice to God," he answers .... A long walk across the thorn-covered roads and the warmth of the noonday sun cause you to question the importance of this trek .... As though reading your thoughts, Jesus responds, "I am glad you joined me today. There are things for you to see and hear. Let these things touch your heart" .... Passing through the city square, bristling with activity, you make your way toward the great Temple .... Jesus quickens his steps as though driven by a power you cannot see .... Cooing doves and restless sheep and goats fill the plaza .... Roughly hewn pushcarts and stalls are crowded together around the Temple steps ....

The moneychangers turn away as you and Jesus pass by .... Two steps at a time, Jesus mounts the stairs .... You feel the heavy pounding of your heart as you attempt to keep up with Jesus' stride .... From the top of the high stairs, the activity taking place around the Temple grounds unfolds .... Men dressed in turbans and long flowing garments shout for all to hear .... "Goats for sale. Perfect animals for our Lord" .... Grubby hands exchange golden Roman coins from the calloused and weathered hands of the poor, promising good fortune .... For a moment, it reminds you of a carnival midway with hawkers peddling their wares .... Shadows of foreboding loom in the distance ....

Jesus, his face red with rage, pounds his fist against the great Temple pillars .... The force of his wrath causes the walk beneath your feet to crack and crumble .... For this is no ordinary man .... Jesus glances toward you, shocked at the fear shadowing your face .... "My friend," he speaks firmly, "come here! Look about you, what do you see?" (*Pause briefly.*) A small child, clothed only in dirt and rags, pulls at your clothing begging for food. Tears of hunger and a swollen belly tell his story .... The crippled beggar kneels before the Temple steps. In disgust and embarrassment, the rich merchants pelt him with spittle and animal dung ....
A moneychanger laughingly wrestles a woman's small bag of coins from her grasp .... Jesus cries, tears stinging his contorted face .... "I cannot watch injustice and do nothing. There is no room in my Father's house for such as this! Go quickly and gather pieces of rope from the animal stalls" ....

Jesus takes the rope from your hands and quickly weaves it into a long whip with brutal barbed ends .... "Stay here, friend. I must clean my Father's house" .... With the fury of a hurricane, Jesus thrashes out against the wrongdoers again and again, sending the animals scurrying to freedom .... The rope sings its cruel whistle .... Golden coins fall to the ground, only to be eaten by the goats .... You stand beneath the branches of a tree .... For this is a Jesus you did not know .... You have always pictured a smiling face, love-filled eyes, and children gathered around his feet .... The animals are gone, the pushcarts and stalls in disarray .... A quiet fills the air .... Jesus has cleared the Temple .... You tremble in fear of this unknown Jesus ....

The Jewish leaders gather in small groups of angry-tongued men .... Jesus sighs heavily and slides down the trunk of the tree .... Sitting on the green knoll, he leans against the tree's gnarled trunk .... "Child, do not be afraid" .... Patting the ground, he motions for you to sit next to him .... You stand in place .... "My Father's house is no longer a marketplace and the hungry shall be fed. Do not feel fear, for I love you. I banished these people because they pretend to live by God's laws. It is not always going to be enough to speak of injustice. There are times you must take a stand for what is right and just. Silence is not golden; it is only an escape" .... Reaching out, he places his hands on your eyes, "Your eyes are for seeing truth, not for looking away" .... Jesus wipes a tear from his cheek and places his hand on top of yours .... You gently slide down beside him .... His sweaty palm and heaving chest tell you of the agony of his decision .... Draw a cloth from your pocket .... You wipe his forehead .... Jesus smiles faintly and takes a deep breath .... "My friend, are there not situations in your own life that you have turned away from rather than try to right? .... Is there someone in your workplace who strives to climb the ladder of success, only to trample those in his or her path? .... Do you remain silent when others poke fun at gays, blacks, or Latinos? (*Pause briefly after each question.*) Do you cast your vote for the political salesman who advocates abortions for the poor, the death penalty, or euthanasia for the old and infirm? .... Does living in public housing mean living with rats and crime-filled streets? .... Is it easier for your to close your eyes than see the gangs that exist in your child's school? .... Talk to me, my child." *(Pause.)*

I will leave you for a moment so that you may speak with Jesus.

Prayer

Heavenly Father, open my eyes and my heart that I may see the world's cruelties and the pain of injustice. Let me move beyond seeing, move me to action that will better the situation. Let my heart feel the pain of hunger, the agony of homelessness, the conflict of parents and children trying to do the right thing, let me feel your pain. I pray that I may become part of the solution rather than another problem. Amen.

As the sun lowers itself below the housetops, it is time for you to leave .... Tell Jesus good-bye for now .... Carry his message in your heart .... Walk down the cobblestone path, open your eyes, and return to this room.

Discussion

In the whole group, discuss the following questions:

- If this were your first encounter with Jesus, how would you feel now?
- Who are the poor and the oppressed in our world today?
- What are *you* doing to make justice a reality for them?
- If you were to bring a symbolic sacrifice to the altar of God, what would that be?

Closing Prayers

Ask for prayer petitions. Pray the Lord's Prayer and Glory Be.

Response: Lord, hear our prayer.

Part 3

Period Of Purification And Enlightenment

Triduum: A Time for Prayer, a Time for Sorrow, a Time for Joy

In the meditations of the Triduum, you will have the
opportunity to walk with Jesus during his final hours. You will
experience the humility of servitude, the realization of denial,
and Christ's final breaths of life. Soon you will stand before
the Church to receive the promise of baptism, the bread of life
within the holy Eucharist, and the gift of the Spirit of God in
confirmation. May this be the beginning of your walk with
Christ. Remember these final hours well for they are truth;
they tell the story of the paschal mystery.

Catechumenate Retreat Day

If you do a retreat day for those about to celebrate the
sacraments of initiation, the reflections on pages 124–139 will
help the candidates and the catechumens participate in the
Vigil Mass in a personal and prayerful way.

The reflections are based on the readings from the Easter Vigil
Mass. These reflections differ from the meditations in this
book, consisting of Scripture readings, prayers, and activities
instead of guided meditations. They include several possibilities
for sponsors to share with the group prior to private prayer or
activities.

The Scripture readings for each reflection should be read in
their entirety. You may want to highlight particular verses for
emphasis. If you cannot fit all the readings into your time frame,
choose those that will be most meaningful for your group.

Planning the Catechumenate Retreat Day

Invite sponsors and other lay leaders to help prepare for this retreat day. Plan to hold your retreat at a place that has both indoor and outdoor facilities. Plan a casual day of relaxation and prayer.

Supplies

- Music selections on tape (or a volunteer to supply guitar or piano accompaniment)
- Bell to signal time or meals
- Bibles
- Pencils

Retreat Day Opening Prayer and Introduction

Lord, we gather together on this day to walk through the unending pages of time; the Word of God breathes life within us. As you healed the blind man, also open our eyes and hearts to the world around us. As you forgave the woman at the well, forgive our sins and send us out into the world to preach your Good News. Awaken our Spirits as you awakened Lazarus, so that we may come closer to you each day. Guide us on our journey this day and all the days of our lives. Amen.

During the season of Lent and the celebration of Easter, God continues creating through us. Once there was the darkness of sin and despair; now there is the light of Christ. We shall experience a renewed life through Christ. Don't expect this to happen overnight. The creation of our new life in Christ takes time, but God will see how good it is and will shout from the mountaintop, "It is good!"

A Time of Discernment

And the Lord spoke, I have called you by name; you are mine. Do not fear, for I am with you (Isa 43:1–4).

The rite of election marks the final stage in the journey toward the Easter Vigil Mass, your baptism. This is the time for you to meet your God face-to-face. It is also a time of discernment: Do I feel the call of God? How do I know Jesus? Am I worthy of this step? Will I be faithful in my future life? The answers of which are known only to you and your Lord.

The following meditation does not tell a story; its message is a private conversation between you, God the Father, God the Son, and God the Holy Spirit. Rest in his love. Hear his voice. The Holy Spirit shall lie within.

Meditation

Find a comfortable position .... Close your eyes .... Center yourself in the eyes of God .... A wave of calm settles upon you .... Refreshing you in the Spirit .... Shut away the cares and sounds of the day .... It is only you and your Lord .... Breathe in his love .... Breathe out the love of Christ ....

You have come to your favorite spot .... The warmth of a spring sun loosens the muscles in your back and neck .... Jesus sits nearby .... There is a presence of calm .... A presence of love .... Jesus rises, sipping from a gourd filled with mountain water .... He offers you a drink .... Slowly the water slides down your throat .... "You shall never thirst again, my friend," Jesus comments .... Brushing his hair aside, he once again takes his seat near you .... Jesus speaks your name .... "My friend, your godparents and the assembly have spoken out in favor of you .... You are about to enter God's own Church .... I shall place these questions upon your heart .... Dwell in them .... Speak only to me ....

- "Have you listened carefully to God's word? Did these words become a living testimony of my presence? (*Pause.*)

- Look within your heart .... You have heard my call .... Are you ready to enter the life of my Church, through the sacraments?

- Are there questions that remain unspoken? (*Pause.*)

- Do you believe that I can be found in the rich and the poor, the outcast, the homeless, the prisoner, the drunk, the junkie? (*Pause.*)

- Can even the ignorant show you the face of God? (*Pause.*)

I will leave you to spend this time with your Lord ....

Jesus stands, his arms outstretched .... Walk into his arms .... The sweet fragrance of rose blossoms wafts in the soft breeze of springtime .... Jesus asks you to kneel before him .... He removes his cloak and spreads it upon the ground .... Feel the coarseness of the weave beneath you .... The gentleness of a caring Lord .... First, Jesus places his hands on your shoulders, pressing lightly .... Can you feel his touch? .... Raising his arms in prayer, he begins his blessings over you, "May you find joy in daily prayer. Through prayer you shall grow closer to me .... Read the Word of God, dwell upon it in your heart .... May you acknowledge your faults and work wholeheartedly to correct them .... May you abstain with courage from everything that defiles your heart" .... Jesus takes your hands in his, helping you to your feet .... The sun plays hide-and-seek with the shadows .... Jesus continues, "May you grow to love and seek righteousness of life, renounce your self, putting others first .... May you share with others the joy you have found in your faith" ....

Jesus takes a ragged cloth from his pocket, spilling water from the gourd upon it; he gently strokes your forehead .... Drops of water flow down your cheeks .... They moisten your lips .... Jesus closes his eyes in reverence .... He silently

makes the sign of the cross above your head .... He speaks his
final prayer:

> *My dear friend, you have set out with me on the road*
> *that leads to the glory of Easter. I will be your way,*
> *your truth, and your life. Until we meet again for the*
> *scrutinies, walk always in my peace.*

I will give you a moment to dwell in the Lord ....

It is time to take your leave .... Turn and walk down the
rugged path .... The road lies ahead .... The journey
awaits .... Open your eyes and return to this room.

Discussion

- What did you see? What did you hear?
- If you could keep one moment or one prayer forever on
  your heart and lips, what would it be?

Closing

Pray the Glory Be in echo form.

Rite of Election

Your ways, O Lord, are love and truth to those who keep your covenant.

Scripture: Mt 4:1–11; Mk 1:12–15; Lk 4:1–13
Feast: 1st Sunday of Lent (A)
Music Suggestion: any selection from *Dream Journey* or "When You Seek Me"/*Gentle Sounds*

The second step in Christian initiation is called both election and enrollment of names. This will close the time of formation of your minds and hearts. This celebration usually coincides with the beginning of Lent. This is also a time for intense preparation for the sacraments. The readings for this day are rich in the symbolism of water and God's covenant with us.

Today's Gospel reading speaks of not just the temptation of Jesus but also the choices he has been given. In the first reading of the day (Gn 2:7–9; 3:1–7, cycle A), we explore our creation and the goodness that was formed within us when God stepped forth and breathed the "breath of life" into Adam. Adam's life was rooted to God as is ours. Adam was given choices. He chose wrongly. We are given this same choice: to follow our Lord across the desert.

The Gospels of Matthew, Mark, and Luke all tell us that Jesus spent forty days in the desert soon after his baptism. This was a period of fasting for Jesus. He ate nothing from sunrise until sundown. Jesus endured this fast as a form of prayer, asking his Father's guidance. Yes, even Jesus had to pray for guidance. Is there a message here for us?

Jesus, the Son of Man, experienced all the anxieties and fears, even the temptations that we would encounter. Satan tried to seduce Jesus when he seemed to be at his weakest. Satan took one look at Jesus and thought, "This guy is tired, hungry, confused and pretty miserable. Now is the time to pull out all the stops." What easy prey we must be.

Please, make yourself comfortable, release your imagination .... Allow your body to relax .... Feel the day's tensions leave your body .... Close your eyes and journey into the desert with Jesus.

Meditation

The desert sands sweep across the arid land, forming funnels of earth that rise into the red sky .... Jesus walks ahead, unaware of your presence .... Hunger grips your stomach .... The sun's rays create a haze over the endless miles of sand .... Heat waves rise on the crest of the distant hills .... Jesus suddenly stops short, falling onto the hot sand .... Carrying a small flask of water, you run to his side .... He doesn't seem to see you; he sits motionless .... His lips are cracked and bleeding from the sun .... Wet a small handkerchief with drops of the precious life-giving water .... Press it against Jesus' lips .... For an instant he holds your hand to his lips ....

The sky darkens .... Ill winds blow .... An image stands before you .... Not man, not beast .... His lips curved in a knowing smile .... Jesus rises, pushing himself between you and this vision of temptation .... You are an observer, nothing else .... You are powerless to move or to make a decision .... A taunting voice of evil speaks, "If you truly are the Son of God, tell these stones to become bread" .... Jesus wipes the particles of sand from his parched lips and replies, "Man does not live on bread alone, but on every word that comes from the mouth of God" .... Angered by this, Satan wraps an arm around Jesus, whisking him away from harsh reality ....

Satan takes Jesus to the highest point in the holy city, the Temple .... You follow in the evil hurricane of promised destruction. Satan leans close to the ear of Jesus, "If you are the Son of God," he says, "throw yourself down" .... With a hand on Jesus' back, pushing, nudging toward the edge of the building, Satan continues, "For it is written: God will command his angels in all that concerns you, and they will lift you up in their hands so that you will not strike your foot against a stone. Jump, fool, jump!" .... Jesus, growing tired of this assault, answers, "It is also written: 'Do not put the Lord your God to the test'" .... Angered by this rebuttal, Satan once again carries Jesus to the top of the highest mountain .... Jesus stands near the crumbling edge of boulders eaten away by the sea and by time .... Satan orders, "Look below. See all of the kingdoms of the world and all of their splendor. All this I will give to you .... If you will bow down and worship me" ....

Jesus peers far into the valley below and shakes his head, "Away from me, Satan! For it is written, 'Worship the Lord your God and serve him only'" .... In failure and anger, Satan folds into the night sky .... Jesus crumples to his knees in prayer and exhaustion .... Clouds form a protective blanket around him .... Jesus notices you crouched in the mountain grasses .... He smiles, rises, and walks toward you, "It is time to leave this place" .... Placing an arm around your shoulders, he leads you down the mountainside, coming to rest near a small creek .... The waters tumble to the valley below .... Dip your hand into the cool waters .... A sudden spray leaves droplets on your face .... Jesus presses his lips into the bubbling creek .... "My friend, I, too, am not without temptation. These things that you have seen today are no different than the temptations the world offers you. I know that it is often hard to separate the world's pleasures from the goodness of life" .... Jesus settles back, resting against the grassy slope. "The world teaches, 'If it feels good, do it.' The world offers only temporary joy while my Father offers life everlasting" .... "Know that I, too, have felt the cold sweat of fear and the pressure of decision. Turn to my Father for protection and guidance. Turn your face toward God, my child." (*Pause briefly.*) Jesus stretches forward, grasping your hands in his, "What are those things that tempt your soul and body, my child? How can I help you?" ....

I will leave you alone with Jesus to talk about this .... Think of the times you find it hardest to resist in following the footsteps of the world .... Let Jesus strengthen you.

Prayer

Jesus, calm my fears, strengthen my spirit. May my walk of life follow your footsteps. Allow me to rest in faith, stand with you beside me, and walk forever in your guiding light. Amen.

Group Discussion

• Where are you most vulnerable to temptation?

• Have you ever found yourself in the "desert" of your life?

Prayer Service

Supplies: paper, pencils, petri dish, background music

Optional: small amount of sand or kitty litter for bottom of dish

Pass out paper and pencils. Ask the group to think in silence of those things that cause the most concerns or problems in their lives—perhaps an area that needs strengthening. Have them write those concerns or problems on the slips of paper, and then fold them up. Then, one person at a time, they can drop the folded papers into the petri dish in the order they feel comfortable with. Remain in silence. Kneel, holding hands, and pray the Our Father.

The Cloak of God

Scripture: Mk 9:2–10; Lk 9:28–36a
Feast: 2nd Sunday of Lent (ABC)
Music Suggestion: any selection from *Dream Journey*

As Americans we spend a great deal of our lives looking forward to the next best thing that will happen. In the Third World countries that might be having a full stomach. The television and movie screens tease us with sneak previews of coming attractions. These previews usually whet our appetites for more, don't they? Jesus also resorted to offering a preview, something to get our interest aroused.

Many Jewish people, including the apostles, were expecting a political Messiah. Because Jesus wasn't a political leader, he used events to tell the apostles that he was indeed the Messiah. With Jesus' death in the near future, the apostles needed reassurance that Jesus was the Messiah and the kingdom of God on earth was at hand. So he offered them a preview of what the kingdom of God would be like after the resurrection. But seeing is not always believing.

After having traveled for six exhausting days through the villages around Philippi, Jesus invited Peter, James, and John to join him in climbing to the top of a large mountain. This was not exactly what they wanted to do right then. The reluctant band of men set out on a trek that would span decades of time. Let's free our imaginations, joining Jesus and his friends in what turned out to be an amazing journey.

Meditation

Find a comfortable position .... Close your eyes .... Feel your arms and hands relax .... The cares of the day shift into

79

nothingness .... Take a deep breath in .... Slowly exhale ....
Whisper "Jesus" ....

You are climbing a very steep hill .... The muscles in your legs
burn with each push forward. Your foot slips on a rolling
stone .... The sun's rays beat down your back .... Beads of
perspiration fall from your brow .... Jesus walks ahead of you,
taking two steps at a time .... Jesus turns and motions for you
to hurry .... James sits down on a weathered tree stump,
trying to catch his breath .... Peter, the oldest, pushes past
you to speak with Jesus .... Listen to Peter's puffing and
panting .... You smile to yourself .... Jesus calls back to you,
"Did you ever see a more beautiful day?" .... "May we stop for
a while?" you ask .... "We'll soon be at the top," Jesus
responds with a tinge of irritation .... Pausing momentarily,
Jesus comments, "My father must become very annoyed.
People are in such a hurry to get where they are going that
they forget where they have been and where they are" ....

At long last you arrive at the mountain's crest .... It is almost
flat .... Huge boulders of rocks burst free of the mountain's
grasp, casting long shadows in the moonlight .... The winds
blow your hair, blushing your cheeks with its cool breath ....
Jesus drops to his knees and begins to pray .... Looking over
his shoulder, Jesus speaks to you and to his disciples, "Join
me now in prayer, giving thanks to God for our many
blessings." (*Pause briefly.*) Peter murmurs, "It's about time we
rest," as he drops to the ground, folding his legs beneath
him .... Soon everyone falls asleep except you and Jesus ....
You bow your head in prayer ....

Feel the presence of a warm glow .... Look up. You are
bathed in a light that is as bright as the sun .... Cup your
hands over your eyes .... Jesus remains kneeling, radiant in
the light .... His clothing takes on a luminescent glow .... You
turn to see Jesus speaking with two men .... They are old and
feeble; they did not make this journey with you .... Peter
wakes out of a deep slumber, his mouth wide open at the
wonder of what he sees before him .... He cries out, "It is
Moses and Elijah. They have returned from the dead!"

17. The Cloak of God

Jesus speaks to Elijah, the prophet of Jesus' coming who foretold Jesus' birth, and with God's favored leader, Moses .... Strain to hear what they are saying .... The three men of God discuss how Jesus is going to die in Jerusalem .... Can you hear them? .... You shudder, knowing these words are not for your ears .... Your heart pounds with fear .... Peter's mouth moves a mile a minute, talking on and on about putting up some kind of buildings, shelter for the visitors .... James covers his eyes, shielding them from the lights .... John whispers in your ear, "It is all right to be afraid. Peter feels it. He just doesn't always know what else to do or say, so he keeps on talking. Do you ever do this?"

In an instant the shadow of a cloud appears and covers everyone with its soft, billowing arms .... You cannot see above or below .... There is just the cloud .... Even Peter sits in silence now .... A deep voice comes from the cloud, "This is my Son, whom I love. Listen to him" .... The voice of God is not silent, clouds drift from the face of the moon .... You huddle together with the disciples, speaking of what you have just seen ....

In the shadows of the evening, your party makes its way down the mountainside. Loose rocks cause you to stumble .... Jesus catches you in his arms .... You start to question the events of the night, but Jesus places his finger across his lips, "Shh!" ....

Eventually, Jesus stops by a clump of trees to rest, inviting you to join him .... He speaks softly, his words carried on the gentle breeze of night, "The days that are yet to come will bring pain to my body and my Spirit. The very ones who have seen the miracles, and walked with us to this mountaintop will not be at my side for my last hours. Only one will be faithful to the end .... Instead they will lock themselves in a darkened room. Fear will rule their hearts .... Jesus rests his head in his hands, his voice quivers, "Those who should believe will falter. The rich man cared more for his wealth than my promises. Yet, the Samaritan women will forever tell my story" .... Jesus places his hand on your shoulder, "You have walked with me this day; you have experienced the wonders of this night. Will your footsteps lead you to my cross? .... Will you hide in the darkness of life, locking your heart to the suffering and pain around you? .... Peter will live to deny me, will you also? .... Will you place your life in my hands and in my heart?"

I will leave you alone with Jesus .... Look into your heart and answer Jesus. (*Pause for one minute or until the group grows restless.*)

Prayer

Dearest Jesus, I stand humbly before you. I have difficulty understanding what you want of me. How may I serve you, Lord? Bless me with the wisdom to know what you ask of me. Fill me with faith, faith enough to reach beyond myself to serve you. Amen.

Discussion

- Has there been a time in your life when you felt the presence of God in a special way?
- How could the experience of the transfiguration help the apostles to understand Jesus as the Messiah?

Closing

Dim the lights. Light a candle. Play background music.

Just as Jesus stood on the mountaintop asking you to slow down and look around you, Jesus now asks that you think of the gifts and the blessings of your life. Spend time in silent prayer giving thanks to God. (*Allow three to five minutes.*)

Close with either individual prayer petitions or a group Glory Be to the Father.

Wells of Wonder, Wells of Hope

Scripture: Jn 4:5–15,19–30
Feast: 3rd Sunday of Lent (A)
Music Suggestion: any selection from *Dream Journey*

The meditation, reflective prayer, and closing prayer are designed to be used together or separately depending upon your needs.

Have you ever been surprised by a random act of kindness? Recently, I found myself lost in a very poor neighborhood of Portland, Oregon. The sun was quickly leaving the city's horizon, being replaced with glowing neon lights and Closed signs. The city streets were littered with empty wine bottles, crushed cigarette butts, and broken dreams. My big white car did nothing to hide me from the ravages of the city. I was sincerely fearful as drunken men and homeless souls held out their hands for the few cents I held in my purse. Feeling hopelessly lost and terrified, I was startled to the point of tears when a fist pounded on my car top. I was afraid to look out the window and see my fate. The pounding was relentless. A woman's voice called out, "Honey, git your white tail out of here. This place ain't safe for your kind." Without waiting for my stammered response the middle-aged woman, dressed in a ragged but clean topcoat, continued, "Go down two blocks and turn right, then drive straight out of here!" Almost as an afterthought, she added, "God Bless you!" I have asked myself many times if I would have stopped for her had the positions been reversed. I hope so. I believe that God sends these messengers of faith into our lives. Perhaps it serves as a wake-up call to remind us that regardless of a person's appearance or ethnic background, God's love falls on everyone. God loves for the sake of loving.

In the time of Jesus the Samaritans were the despised, falling to the level of dogs. Samaritans were half Jewish and half Assyrian, the conquering heroes of the battle for the northern Jewish kingdom. Some stayed and married Jewish women to live in the country of Samaria. They were considered half-breeds, being neither Jew nor Assyrian. Jews and Samaritans rarely spoke to each other, fearing the wrath of their community. Women were on an even lower level of acceptance, with Jewish men thanking God in their prayers that they were not born as a lowly woman. Rabbis often debated if women indeed had a soul.

Jesus made every effort to break down this wall of prejudice based on lack of knowledge and love of fellow men—and women. Jesus brought living water to the Samaritans through the telling of God's story. He offered hope where there was none. He offered the wonder of life everlasting. God's love for us is manifest in Jesus Christ.

Meditation

Find a comfortable position …. Close your eyes …. Allow your arms and legs to relax …. The sounds around you slowly fade away …. Take a deep breath …. Let it out slowly …. Whisper "Jesus" …. Find the calm in the center of your being ….

The summer sun lies midway in the blue sky above …. The warm rays of light nearly blind you …. The long walk across the desert lands has dried your throat and mouth …. Your lips are blistered and peeling …. Water—you must have a drink from the village well …. All you can think about is a cool, refreshing drink of water ….

Quickly, you make your way down the winding path to the well …. A lone man sits by the side of the well …. To your surprise, it is Jesus! …. He looks up with a nod, and announces, "There is no dipper for the water. Come and wait with me; someone will come along soon and give us a drink" …. Your eyes meet briefly …. A cloud of dust billows about his sandaled feet ….

You grow tired of sitting in the hot sun …. Your mouth feels drained of moisture as though it is filled with cotton balls …. Jesus notices your impatience. "Someone is coming this way as we speak" …. A woman from the neighboring village appears by the side of the well. She is startled by the presence of Jesus and you ….

Jesus speaks to the woman, "Would you be so kind as to give us a drink from the well?" …. The young woman with long black curls stands with her mouth open in shock …. "You are a Jew. Why do you ask me, a Samaritan woman, for a drink?" …. Jesus startles her by answering, "If you knew who I am you would ask me to give you *living water* so that you would never thirst again" …. *"Living water?"* she mutters …. Shaking her head, she lowers the bucket into the well …. Jesus stands, adjusting his rope belt. "Anyone who drinks from this well will be thirsty again. If you only knew what a wonderful gift God has for you, and who I am, you would ask me for *living water*" …. The woman's dark eyes widen. "But you don't have a rope or a bucket. Where do you expect to get this living water?".... Jesus smiles …. "The water I offer will become a constant spring within, watering you, refreshing you forever with eternal life, never to thirst again."

The woman slowly fills a cup from her bucket …. Carefully studying Jesus, she asks, "Who are you? Are you a prophet?" …. A summer wind sends twisting coils of sandy earth twirling across the courtyard …. Jesus shakes his head slightly, brushing his hair aside. He sips the cool water from the cup; then, handing the cup to you, he smiles and gestures for you and the woman to sit down with him …. You place your back against the ancient well …. Jesus tells her, "Go and get your husband" …. The woman responds quickly, "But I am not married." Jesus looks deep within her being. "All too true! You have had five husbands and you are not even married to the man you are living with now" …. The woman gasps, placing a hand over her mouth. "You are a prophet! What is your name?" ....

Jesus speaks to the woman of many things about her past but never condemns her .... You feel the embarrassment of hearing more than you wanted to .... Placing one hand on your shoulder, Jesus looks intently into your eyes, "The message I bring to this woman is also for your ears and for your heart .... Always speak to God with an honest heart. Ponder on the word of God. Learn to know me, your Lord, for I have come to save what was lost .... Review your life before me and humbly acknowledge your sins."

Leaving the woman to ponder on this, he takes your hands in his and, in his low, gentle voice, speaks to you, "My Father loves you. The love of God is not based on what you do, how you do it, or how you lived in the past .... God loves for the sake of loving. His love is the wellspring of life .... Rest in his grace, my child. Allow God to carry your burdens .... Rest in his love." (*Pause briefly.*) Jesus wipes a small tear from your eyes then wraps a loving arm around your shoulders .... "Reach within your sleeping soul and ask the Holy Spirit to awaken your sense of God" .... I will leave you in the quiet of the day for a few moments. (*Pause.*)

Jesus slowly rises, his warm hand still resting on your shoulders, "I am the Messiah. If the *living waters* work through you, you will grow to understand that it should not matter what color a person's skin is or where he calls home .... Within these *living waters* there is hope for everyone. Take moments of your day and invest them in worshiping God. Give thanks for his blessings. Remember to return to this well of hope, this well of God's wonder."

The sun slides beneath the rooftops .... Long fingers of darkness crisscross the courtyard .... Jesus stands, "It is time for both of you to return home" .... The woman gathers her water jug. Jesus places his gentle arms around her, then sends her on her way .... "She will lead many others to believe in me" .... Jesus stretches his arms and back; then returning to your resting place, he blesses your forehead, "While you await the gift of God, may you long with all of your heart for the *living waters* that bring eternal life" .... Jesus places his arms around your shoulders, speaking your name. "Will you lead others to believe in me through the example of your life?" ....

I will leave you for a moment so that you can speak to Jesus. (*Pause.*)

Prayer

Lord, you are my eternal source of light, justice, and truth, take me under your tender care. Purify me and make me holy; give me knowledge, sure hope, and understanding. May I be worthy to receive the grace of baptism. May your Holy Spirit fill me with the faith to come before Father God with honesty and hope. Amen.

Tell Jesus good-bye for now .... Walk away slowly .... Turn and look at Jesus once again .... Open your eyes and return to this room.

Discussion

If you are working with a large group, it would be a good idea to break down into groups of four to six for sharing.

- How will you tell someone about the *well of hope—the well of wonder?*

- Share a time or a way in which you are most comfortable and most sincere in *talking* to God.

Reflective Prayer

Dim the lights. Light a candle. Play background music. Place a large bowl of water and a ladle on the table with small cups beside the bowl. Ask the group to spend a few minutes (three to five) in reflection and silent prayer. By example, you may wish to share a portion of your own prayer with the group. This will set the tone.

Slowly read John 12:44–50, pausing briefly at the end of each verse.

- What message do you hear?

Ask the group to join you in the following prayer of faith:

Response: Amen, my Lord. Amen.

Leader: Listen, Israel: I shall love the Lord my God with all my heart (Deut 6:4–5).

Response

Leader: Lord, you have words of everlasting life (Jn 6:68).

Response

Leader: The Gospel will save me only if I believe what is preached to me (1 Cor 15:1–4).

Response

Leader: God loved the world so much, he gave his only Son, that all who believe in him might have eternal life (Jn 3:16).

Response

Leader: I, the light, have come into the world, so that whoever believes in me need not remain in the dark any more (Jn 12:44–50).

Response

Invite each person to come forward and fill his or her cup with water, a symbol of living water, make the sign of the cross, and offer this prayer:

> *I, (name), drink from the living waters of Christ, my Lord.*

Closing Prayer—The Apostles' Creed

Invite the elect to stand in a circle joining hands. Pray the Apostles' Creed in echo format.

Heal My Spirit, Lord

Scripture: Jn 9:1–41
Feast: 4th Sunday of Lent (A)
Music Suggestion: "When You Seek Me"/*Gentle Sounds*

The Gospel today speaks of light and darkness, sight and blindness. It is a familiar story for most of us, the story of the blind man who, through Christ Jesus, opened his mind and his eyes to see the light of Christ. Although we may not be physically blind, most of us have been spiritually blind at some time in our lives. The readings ask us to look inside our soul, to examine our life. Are we really Christian? Do our priorities and opinions get in the way of taking the appropriate action?

Meditation

Slowly close your eyes .... The familiar will shift from view .... Darkness shadows the light of day. Imagine your world without the gift of sight. (*Pause.*) Yet Jesus speaks to us of a far greater blindness, that of seeing our lives shrouded in darkness .... Let's take a journey into the Gospel of John, joining Jesus as he leaves the Mount of Olives and the Temple courtyard behind him. The legalistic Pharisees have once again turned their backs on truth, on the Son of God.

Find a comfortable position .... Allow your body to slowly relax, starting at your shoulders .... Shut out the sights and sounds around you .... Your arms fall at rest .... Take a deep breath .... Let it out slowly .... Whisper "Jesus" ....

Chill winds sweep across the desert, pausing to strip the land of warmth .... The day draws to a close, the Sabbath is near, and the journey is never-ending .... Jesus walks beside you in silence, his head lowered to his chest .... His steps

89

determined .... You shiver with cold, holding your arms tight to your body .... Barely past the time of winter, grains of sand race with the wind, stinging your legs .... Jesus pulls a woven blanket from his shoulders, draping it across your back .... Small clusters of people are on the roadway ahead .... They look to be derelicts and cripples .... An old man falls in a drunken stupor. They thrust their dirty hands in your path, begging .... Do you turn away? (*Pause.*)

Jesus stops, offering food for the soul. He turns to you, pointing to the pitiful figure of a man groping his way through the crowd. "Is this not the man who has been blind since birth? .... Peter, believing that all pain and suffering is due to sin, speaks up quickly, "If this man has been blind since birth, who is the sinner, his parents or him?" .... Jesus shakes his head in despair .... Not waiting for a reply, Peter rubs his hands over his straggly red beard and orders, "Jesus, do not stop here!" .... Jesus, speaking loud enough for Peter to hear, if indeed he is listening, looks to you, "This man's blindness has happened so that the work of God may be evidenced. Go, my friend and bring the man to me" ....

Make your way to the edge of the road. The crowd separates, circling the fragile young man .... His arms and legs are covered with sores; his frame is skeletal. Sightless eyes are buried in deep caverns .... Take the man by the arm, helping him to his feet .... Dirt and filth blotch his skin .... In fear of the unknown and the shadows of night, you half-carry, half-lead the man to Jesus .... Jesus motions for the disciples to gather round.

"The guy stinks. Let me outa here!" grumbles Peter, quickly moving to the background .... Jesus looks at Peter with disbelief, then lowers himself to the ground .... Taking a handful of dirt he mixes his saliva into the soil, making mud, then covers the man's eyes with the mud, saying to him, "Go now and wash your eyes in the Pool of Siloam and you shall be able to see" .... The man now guided by the hopefuls and the curious, makes his way to the Pool .... Jesus wipes his hands clean of the mud, "This man shall be questioned by many. The Pharisees will not believe, but the man will grow in faith. He may not understand who I am at first, but he shall come to proclaim that I am the light of the world" ....

With the dawning of a new day, Jesus stretches, his arms raised to the sun .... He nudges your side with his foot, "The day begins and the truth of my words will come soon" .... Once again, the small band of men continues the journey of faith .... By midday, you spot the figure of the young blind man. He waves excitedly .... Jesus leads you toward the young man .... "Do you believe in the Son of Man?"Jesus questions .... Stuttering, the man answers, "Who is that, sir? Tell me and I will believe" .... Jesus pats him on the back and smiles. "You are seeing him now; he is the one speaking to you" .... The man falls to the ground, "Lord, I do believe" .... Jesus sends the man on his way to carry the message of hope to all that he shall meet ....

"My child, you have seen the miracles, you have experienced the unexplainable, and you have felt the comfort of my love" .... Jesus motions for you to join him in the shade of a tree .... "Always remember that I am the light in your life. Rest in my Spirit and we shall pray together. I pray to my Father that you will you trust in my truth, preserving it always. (Pause briefly.) Put all fear behind you and go forward with confidence. (Pause briefly.) Allow yourself to be transformed in the Spirit, seeking those things that are holy and just. (Pause briefly.) When you are faced with the values of the world, remain faithful to the spirit of the Gospel. As a child of God, can you openly admit your weaknesses and faults? Speak to me, my child." I will give you a few minutes to share with Jesus. (Pause.)

Prayer

Dearest Lord, Create in me a new heart and a new spirit. Grant me your pardon and your peace that I may serve you. Lead me from darkness into your unfailing light, that I may give witness to the faith. You are Lord forever and ever. Amen.

A tear forms on Jesus' cheek .... Gently, wipe away his tears .... Jesus smiles warmly and holds you in his arms for a moment, then he releases you to go forward on your journey of life .... Jesus steps backward, gazing at you intently, then places both his hands on top of your head in prayer, "May God dispel darkness and be the light that shines in your heart. Gently lead others to me, for I am the *light of the world* .... You have been enlightened by the Holy Spirit. May you never fail to profess the Good News of salvation and share it with others .... I pray that by the example of your life, you may become in me, Jesus Christ, the *light of the world*." (*Pause.*)

It is time for you to return .... Jesus wraps his arms around you, sending you on your way with the strength of his love and the Spirit of God glowing in your heart .... Open your eyes and return to this room.

Discussion

- Have you ever carried the burden of believing that unfortunate things happen to those who have sinned? Has this caused you to take the responsibility for all of your family's tough breaks?

- If you were questioned concerning your faith with the intensity of the Pharisees, what would you say?

- When did Jesus become the *light of your world*?

Closing Prayer

Supplies: votive candles for each person, a large candle, background music, small paper cups

Dim the lights, light the large candle, and play background music. Create a focal point by placing a Bible open to John 9 on the table near the candle.

Ask the group to spend a few minutes (one to three) in silent prayer. At the close of silent prayer, ask each one to come forward and light a votive candle from the flame of the large candle, placing it in the paper cups. Offer the following prayer petitions.

Response: Lord, hear our prayer.

Leader: May we always trust in the truth of Christ, finding freedom of mind and heart, let us pray to the Lord.

Response

Leader: May we always remain faithful to the Spirit of the Gospel, let us pray to the Lord.

Response

Invite prayer petitions.

Close by praying the Lord's Prayer in echo format.

The Death and Life Of Lazarus

Scripture: Jn 11:1–44
Feast: 5th Sunday of Lent (B)
Music Suggestion: "We Believe in You"/*Gentle Sounds*

What emotions are stirred when I bring up the topic of death? Are you uneasy? sad? Are memories hiding beneath the surface of your life?

The loss of a loved one leaves emptiness and feelings of abandonment. Tears still burn behind my eyes when I think of the loss of my daughter. The death of a pet will bring strong emotion to most of us. Until my daughter died, I had walked through life feeling that death was something that would always happen to someone else.

If I were to ask you to describe Jesus, would that description include his ability to cry, to feel the pain of loss? Most of us think of Jesus as being strong, as having the ability of knowing the outcome of every situation. Perhaps strength includes the ability to feel the sadness of tears.

Jesus, wishing his followers to experience God's presence and the transformation of death to hope, allowed certain events to follow their true course. The illness and death of Lazarus were to be a manifestation of God's glory, not the story of a friend helping a friend. Jesus enjoyed the friendship of Martha and Mary, her sister, and that of their brother, Lazarus. They often broke bread together and shared stories of the glory of God. Theirs was a friendship rivaling that of siblings. Lazarus and Jesus undoubtedly spent time in a small wooden boat, rocking with the force of the sea, fishing, then sharing the bounty of the sea. The loss of a friend leaves a blueprint of the love that once was. Lazarus became ill and died very suddenly. Martha and Mary sent a pleading message for Jesus to return, for they knew that the power of God would restore Lazarus' health. But Jesus chose instead to continue on his journey of ministry. "Why?" is the most frequently asked question concerning this story. Let's release our imaginations, joining Jesus on the opposite side of the Jordan River, in the land where John the Baptist once preached.

Meditation

Find a comfortable position .... Close your eyes .... Feel the muscles in your arms and legs relax .... Find the calm in the center of your being .... Take a deep breath .... Let it out slowly, whisper "Jesus" ....

You are sitting among the tall blades of grass carpeting the hillside .... Rays of the sun warm the back of your neck .... Children play nearby with a ball made of goatskin .... The ball slowly rolls across the grass, coming to a stop at your feet .... You toss the ball back to the waiting children .... Glancing over your shoulder, you see that Jesus is surrounded by people .... Some stretch their arms forward to touch even the hem of his garment .... A messenger breaks through the multitude, handing a rolled message to Jesus .... Jesus reads, frowns, and, letting out a deep sigh, places the scroll in the sleeve of his robe, continuing to minister to the crowds .... Peter, knowing the message, casts a worried look at Jesus .... Jesus, sensing this, speaks to you and Peter, "Lazarus will not die, my friends" ....

For two more days you stay by Jesus' side as he reaches out to those in need .... Jesus, always compassionate and kind, appears to have forgotten the illness of his friend. During the early evening hours of the second day, Jesus turns to you and announces, "It is time to make our way to the home of Lazarus. He has fallen asleep and I will awaken him" .... The disciples prepare for the journey, packing bread and dried fish into knapsacks. There is a great deal of talk among the men .... You sit in silence, listening as the men scold Jesus with their tone.

As you begin the long journey to Bethany, Jesus places his hand on your shoulder to steady his tired steps .... Stones on the pathway cut through the soles of your thin sandals .... Jesus seems not to notice .... Through the night, the cluster of men plod on to their destination .... Jesus walks in silence, his head heavy upon his chest .... On the second day of this journey, dust from the well-traveled road rises with the dawn .... Beyond the funnels of rising sand, you notice a woman running toward you .... The brightness of the early morning sun forms a shroud of light about her shoulders .... She waves her arms frantically. Without looking up, Jesus speaks, "It will be Martha" ....

According to the mideastern culture, Martha pulls her veil over her face showing only her red-rimmed eyes, "Lazarus is dead!" she cries .... The words are spit out rapidly; peppered with anger and grief .... The group comes to a halt; sighs of pain and loss fill the air. Peter accuses Jesus with his eyes ....
A low grumble echoes among the men .... Martha once again assaults Jesus with her words. "If you had been there, maybe my brother would still be alive!" ....

Jesus reaches through her pain, taking her into his loving arms .... "Do not worry. Your brother will live again for I am the source of all life," he tells her .... "But, Jesus," you interrupt, thinking he had forgotten, "Lazarus is dead!" "Trust me," Jesus states firmly .... Peter speaks in a low, guttural growl, the words unintelligible.

Jesus walks with an arm around Martha, almost pushing her to take the steps forward on your journey. She pulls away, not wanting to look upon his face .... The size of the band grows with each turn in the road. Some come to mourn Lazarus, others to observe Jesus; others walk in the shadows, hoping the worst will come to pass .... Toward the end of the day, you approach the site of Lazarus' tomb .... The hillside is filled with large boulders and barren soil .... Nearing the crest of the hill there is a cave protected with a large stone placed at the entrance ....

Martha tells Jesus that the tomb lies ahead, holding the body of her brother .... Friends and family have gathered at the tomb .... Mary, the younger sister, runs to Jesus' side, pushing you into the background .... Andrew whispers, "Mary is a woman of great faith, but her anguish is a heavy burden" .... The slim young woman with flowing red hair breaks into tears .... "Why didn't you come right away?" she cries .... Mary buries her head in her hands and sobs ....

Your eyes sting with tears .... Have there been times that you felt your prayers weren't answered? (*Pause briefly.*) Sadness darkens the dawn .... Jesus looks toward you, his gaze filled with pain and anguish .... He lowers his head, breaking into sobs of uncontrollable grief .... Tears fall freely down his bearded cheeks .... Peter brushes a tear from his own weathered face .... John takes Martha's hands, leading her to the tomb ....

Jesus moves toward a nearby tree .... You follow closely behind him .... Placing his hands on the massive trunk, Jesus presses his head into the bark of the tree, continuing to sob .... Reaching out for the comfort of your love, Jesus takes your hand in his .... Feel his sorrow .... Wipe away the tears from his eyes .... A teardrop glistens in the early morning light ....

Finally, Jesus is able to speak to Martha and Mary, "I know what is in your heart. Show me where you have laid him" .... Jesus motions for you to follow toward the tomb .... Jesus' strength returns, as he demands of his disciples, "Take away the stone!" .... Martha speaks haltingly, "Oh, no, Lord, there will be a bad odor! He has been there for four days" .... Jesus, ignores her, telling the men, "Put your shoulders against the boulder and move it out of the way" .... Peter's arm muscles strain against the weight of the stone ....

At last, the stone rolls free .... Jesus, his back turned to you, looks toward the heavens, raising his arms in prayer to his Father .... He moves closer to the doorway of the tomb and

commands, "Lazarus, come out!" .... The odor of death fills
the air .... You cover your nose .... Everyone stands in
disbelief and utter silence ....

Has Jesus has gone too far this time? .... Others seem to feel
the same way .... Once again Jesus calls out, "Lazarus, come
here!" .... Low grunts, a stirring, come from within the
tomb .... You move away in fear .... A few moments later,
Lazarus walks from the tomb, his body wrapped in burial
cloths .... Strips of fraying cloth loosen their hold, falling from
his arms and legs .... Lazarus stumbles forward, almost falling
at your feet .... His head is wrapped .... A burial cloth runs
beneath his chin and is tied into a knot on the top of his
head .... The crowd moves back in shock and disbelief ....

Only Martha and Mary rush to embrace Lazarus .... Slowly,
the crowd moves forward, testing the miracle of death to
life .... Lazarus stumbles, then falls .... Shouts of praise ring in
your ears .... "Lazarus lives!" ....

Jesus steps aside and motions for you to follow him .... He
leads you to the shade of an olive tree .... "Do not lie in the
shadow of doubt, my friend. I did not abandon Lazarus, and I
will never abandon you .... Pray with me. Imagine that you
stand before Father God, the source of all life. He knows your
needs, he knows your heart .... Within the silence of your
heart, repeat the words of blessing, the words of need, the gift
of prayer" .... Raising his arms in prayer, Jesus addresses his
Father,

> *Our Father, who is in heaven,*
> *holy is thy name.*
> *May your will be done on earth*
> *as it is in heaven.*

Jesus places one hand on your shoulder, sealing the bonds of
prayer.

Give us this day our daily needs,
those you know better than I.
I thank you, Lord, for the blessing of life,
for hearing our pleading.
Forgive us our sins
and grant that we may forgive those
who bring harm and anger to our lives.
(Pause.)
Lead us not to the temptations of life
and deliver us from all evil. Amen. (Pause.)

Jesus slowly lowers himself to the ground .... His eyes are tired, his spirit strong. He takes your hands in his, "Never turn your back on God when you feel as though your prayers are not answered. It is not God's will that you suffer and die" .... He looks directly into your eyes, speaking in a low, husky voice, "I love you as I have loved Lazarus. I wish to give you new life on earth and everlasting life in heaven" .... You sigh deeply, coming to rest in the warm arms of God. (*Pause briefly.*) Jesus speaks, "You have received the Spirit that makes you God's child and in that Spirit cry out, 'Abba, Father!'" .... Jesus looks upon you intently, "If you could ask one thing of me, what would that be?" .... Jesus waits for your answer.

I will leave you alone for a few moments. Answer Jesus with your heart. (*Pause.*)

Prayer

Jesus, my heart and mind are filled with my own needs. Give me the judgment to know those things that are important and those that my spirit should dismiss. Through your Spirit who gives life, fill me with faith, hope, and charity that I may live with you always in the glory of your resurrection. You are Lord forever and ever. Amen.

The time has come for Jesus to return to his mission .... Jesus steps forward, embracing you in his love .... Turn and walk down the rocky path .... Open your eyes and return to this room.

Discussion

- Is there one thing that happened recently that reminded you of God's presence in your life?
- Have you had an experience or a tough decision to make recently that tested your faith?
- How did God guide and protect you through this difficult time?

Closing Prayer

Music Suggestion: "Only a Shadow"/*Gentle Sounds*

Supplies: tapers or votive candles in paper cups for each person, community candle, background music

Dim the lights, play background music, and light the community candle. Invite three people to alternate reading verses 1–6 of Psalm 23, pausing for reflection and prayer following each verse. It may be helpful to invite sharing which verse meant the most to them at this time and why.

Hail to the King!

Scripture: Lk 22:14–23,56
Feast: Palm/Passion Sunday (ABC)
Music Suggestion: any selection from *Dream Journey*

As we recall the story of Jesus entering the city of Jerusalem humbly riding upon the back of a donkey, we need to also keep in mind the significance of his journey. Depending on who you spoke to, Jesus entered the city gates as a political/military leader, a descendant of King David, and among a few, he was called "Hosanna," a term of prayer bonded with the coming of the Messiah.

Days of glory, nights of whispers, and the pain of death all within the span of nine days. To revel in the glory of his return to Jerusalem was also to feel the sting of a whip, the pain of betrayal, and the ultimate death. Jesus was greeted by the signs of royalty and honor, palm branches usually reserved for conquering armies and kings, were strewn along the road to the city's gates.

Jesus was indeed a hero, but not the one the people of Jerusalem expected. He entered on a donkey's back, a sign of humility, a sign of the burdens he carried.

Meditation

Let's walk with our Lord on this day of triumph for the week will be long and tiring …. Find a comfortable position …. Close your eyes, shutting away the cares of the day …. Relax …. The sounds around you drift into silence …. Your body finds the calm …. Take in a deep breath …. Let it out slowly ….

It is early evening .... You stand by a well-traveled road ....
Clouds of dust rise from the shuffling feet .... Large groups
and families pass by you: the old and infirm, the strong and
sure-footed, the children, innocence on their faces .... It is
time to celebrate Passover .... The hordes are tired, but the air
is filled with excitement and anticipation ... Can you see all
the people? .... Dust blows across the roadway, temporarily
blocking your view ....

The voices grow louder now .... The throngs move to either
side of the roadway .... You can feel the excitement in the
air .... People are murmuring, pushing and shoving to be in
front of the crowd .... The voices are louder now, almost
shouting, "He's coming! Hosanna!"

Push your way through the crowd and climb onto the low
adobe wall that stretches the length of the road .... Can you
see Jesus? .... He is sitting astride a donkey colt; his red cloak
hangs about his shoulders .... People are chanting,
"Hosanna!", a word from the Greek meaning, "Save us, we
pray" .... An old man, thin and fragile with skin of parchment,
places his worn coat in the middle of the thoroughfare ....
Others rush into the confusion, throwing palms in the route of
the visitors .... As Jesus nears, you grasp nearby palm
branches, pushing through the crowd to place them in the
path of the donkey .... You welcome Jesus with your heart ....

The donkey is led by a man with a light brown beard almost
thick enough to cover his youthful face .... You hear Jesus call
him by name, "John" .... As you make your way through the
throng, you pass by several groups of men .... They speak of
politics; they speak of death .... A cold shiver passes through
you .... You must warn him .... Break into a run .... He must
turn away ....

You stand now in front of Jesus .... Feel the warmth of the
donkey's breath on this cool spring day .... John helps Jesus
step from the donkey's back .... You stretch as far as you can
to reach him .... Your fingers touch his cloak .... Can you feel
the roughness of the cloth? .... Jesus turns, he looks right at
you, smiling .... He speaks your name in a voice indicating

surprise .... Can you hear him? .... The crowd forces entry onto the roadway, attempting to get even a glimpse of the man called Jesus .... Two of Jesus' disciples begin to lift him to the back of the colt .... Pull off your own jacket and throw it over the donkey's back to soften his ride .... He does not hear your concern, or perhaps this is inevitable ....

The shouting of the people continues .... Jesus smiles and waves, seemingly carefree, but you feel the burdens of his heart .... You run, you stumble, you keep pace with the entourage .... Jesus leans over and whispers in John's ear .... From the center of the huddle surrounding Jesus, Peter extends his hand to you, placing within your grasp the reins of the donkey .... You lead the colt .... Jesus smiles down at you, placing a hand on your shoulder, "Walk with me, my friend. My journey is almost over" .... A feeling of doom darkens the day .... The crowd begins to cheer .... "Hail to the king!" .... Can you hear the confusion, the noise?

Abruptly, Jesus signals for the parade to stop .... Taking your shaking hand in his, he lifts you onto the donkey's back .... Jesus' arms form a safety net around you .... Loud cheers ring in the air .... Jesus seems not to notice the clamor and noise .... He lowers his head and speaks only to you .... Listen to his words of love .... Jesus asks, "What can I do for you, my child?" .... Welcome Jesus into your heart .... Speak to Jesus from the center of your being .... Welcome Jesus into your life. (*Pause.*)

Prayer

Jesus, allow me to feel the liberation of your death and return to life. Remind me that hardships pass; the glory of God is forever.

I welcome you, Lord, into my life and all that it is and all that it may be. Amen.

In the days to come the hardship of your love will become heavy with grief. But on this day you rode in glory with your Lord. Say good-bye for now .... Turn and walk through the crowds, over the wall .... Open your eyes and return to this room.

The Gentle Touch Of Jesus

Scripture: Jn 13:1–17
Feast: Holy Thursday
Music Suggestion: "I Will Never Forget You"/*Gentle Sounds*

With the dawning of Holy Thursday the Easter Triduum begins. It is a time of prayer and worship. Holy Thursday is referred to as the feast day of the priesthood and of the Eucharist. This evening Mass celebrates Jesus' gift of the holy Eucharist. In memory of Christ's command to serve others as he has served, the celebrant will wash the feet of twelve people, representing Christ's washing of the feet of the Twelve Apostles.

If you knew this was the last day of your life, where would you choose to be? (*Allow time for discussion.*) Jesus knew that in fewer than twenty-four hours he would take his final breath; yet, he chose to spend the last hours of his life teaching his apostles. Unto the end, the evening was not unlike those of the past; it was the celebration of the Passover that brought them together to enjoy each other's fellowship. They dined, sang songs of praise to God, read from the Old Testament, and partook of bread and wine. Then, Jesus knelt on the bare wooden floor before each of his guests and gently washed their feet, the most humble act of servitude.

To better understand this night, let us release our imaginations to join Jesus and his friends on a warm spring evening, for we too shall feel his gentle touch.

You may wish to introduce the following meditation by reading the first paragraph on page 70.

Meditation

Find a comfortable position .... Close your eyes .... Reach for the quiet within .... Shut out the sounds around you .... Take in a deep breath. Whisper "Jesus" .... Let your breath out slowly. Whisper "My Savior" ....

You are sitting around a long table .... women are scurrying about preparing the feast .... The smell of fresh-baked bread fills the small upstairs room. Roast lamb and small red potatoes are carried in on trays .... The room is dim .... The lantern's flickering light bounces off the walls .... Jesus looks drawn with sadness .... He reaches up from his position on the floor pillow, taking your hand in his .... A faint but loving smile crosses his lips .... Judas arrives late, taking his place at the end of the table .... John fills the cups with wine from a goatskin flask .... Wine dribbles onto the tablecloth .... The red stain soaks into the cloth, leaving a pattern of fingers oozing across the table .... Peter hands you an earthenware goblet, nodding his head in welcome.

The room is stilled after Jesus blesses the bread and wine .... He places a small piece of the warm golden bread upon your tongue, saying, "Take this and eat it in remembrance of me" .... Many of the disciples close their eyes, raising their arms toward heaven in prayer .... You hear footsteps behind you .... Quickly glance around .... Judas is slipping out the door .... No one else seems to notice .... A look of pain crosses Jesus' face; he sighs in silent recognition .... Within a short time, everyone is talking at once, each demanding his own time ....

Jesus grasps the edge of the table, pulling himself to his feet .... The room falls silent once again .... He removes his outer garment, takes a towel from a rack and wraps it around his waist; then he removes an empty basin and pitcher from the table .... Jesus hands you the empty pitcher, "Take this and fill it with water and then bring it to me" .... Receiving the roughly hewn pitcher from his hand, you quickly make your way down the stairs, through the yard to the well .... Pulling the bucket of water to the edge of the well, you begin to fill it .... You return quickly to the house, water splashing and spilling onto the floor .... Jesus takes the pitcher from you, wiping the droplets of water from your shirt .... "Thank you, my dear friend," he adds gratefully ....

Jesus hands you a large basin. "I am going to wash the feet of my disciples," he whispers in your ear .... Jesus points to the floor near James's feet .... James stands, placing his hands on the arms of Jesus, "Oh, no, not me, Lord. Call the servant boy if this must be done!" .... Jesus gently persuades James to take his seat and then motions for you to place the bowl on the wood-planked floor .... Water splashes onto the floor, fingers of water stretch forward into the cracks .... You direct James's feet into the basin .... Jesus bends down on one knee, pouring the water over the feet; then taking the towel from his waist, he dries the disciple's feet .... Tears roll down James's cheeks as Jesus has also washed his soul with God's love .... One by one, Jesus leads you around the table, washing each man's feet, then drying them tenderly ....

At last, it is Peter's turn .... Peter stands, then moves backward, stumbling over the floor pillows, insisting, "Lord, you are not going to wash my feet!" .... Jesus glances toward you and then to Peter, explaining, "You do not realize what I am doing, but later you will understand" .... Peter backs into the wall, "You shall never wash my feet!" .... Jesus becomes firm, "Peter, unless I wash your feet, you will have no part of me" .... Peter pulls his feet tightly under the weight of his body. "This is a job for a servant," he protests .... Then reluctantly, he removes his sandals and takes a seat on a wobbly wooden bench .... You place your hands on his roughly calloused feet, lowering them into the bowl .... Particles of sand drift to the top of the bowl .... Peter remains silent, feeling shame that Jesus would crouch on a dirty wooden floor to wash his feet, the feet of a fisherman ....

Jesus rises, taking the bowl from your hands and placing it on the floor .... "I shall wash your feet now" .... You cringe, for now your Lord, the Messiah, kneels before you .... Not waiting for your response, he quickly removes your sandals ....

Softly, gently, he guides your feet into the waiting basin ....
You shiver as a drop of the cold water splashes onto your
leg .... Jesus, the Son of God, the Son of Man, kneels at *your*
feet .... Once again, removing the towel from around his
waist, lifting your feet to his lap, he wraps his towel around
them .... The towel rests warmly upon your feet .... Resting
one elbow on the table, he questions his apostles, "Do you
understand what I have done for you? .... A vague murmur
envelops the table .... "And what about you, my friend?" he
adds, looking deep within your being .... He interrupts your
stammered reply, "You call me 'teacher' and 'Lord,' as you
should for this is what I am" .... His gaze circles the table,
stopping at each man. Noticing the absence of one, he
shudders, then continues, "I have washed your feet, as you
should wash one another's feet" .... Jesus folds the dampened
towels automatically as he speaks, "Do for others as I have
done for you" ....

The room once again buzzes with the drone of the confused
men .... Jesus takes this time to come to your side .... He
folds his legs beneath him, lowering himself onto the floor
once again .... "My child, my friend, you shall be blessed if
you choose to follow me." Placing an arm around your
shoulders, he whispers, "If I were to come into your life this
very day, not this day of the Passover, but this hour, to that
place in your mind and heart, what would you will that I do for
you? (*Pause briefly.*) Would you ask that I hold you in the
safety of my arms? (*Pause briefly.*) Would ask my forgiveness
of your errors in life? (*Pause briefly.*) Where in your life, my
child, do you need to practice foot-washing?"

I will leave you alone with Jesus to answer his questions ....
Remain still and quiet .... Allow only the voice of Jesus to
break through the wall of silence. (*Pause until they appear
restless.*)

Prayer
Lord, wash me clean with the waters of forgiveness.
I often take for granted the love and labors of my
family. I put my job and those I call "friend" in a place

of great importance, forgetting the joy of your gentle touch. Guide me, Lord, that I may follow your footsteps on my journey of faith. Amen.

The time has come to say your good-byes …. It is time to carry this experience with you …. Jesus places his arms around you, sending you on your journey wrapped in his love …. Walk through the door of the upstairs room, walk down the stairs and into this room.

Discussion

Break up into small groups of four to six. Give them a few moments to answer the following questions:

- How has someone you know "washed your feet"?
- With Jesus knowing your every need, how would Jesus "wash" your feet today?

Prayer Service

Bring the group together. Lower the lights using only candlelight. Play background music. Explain that each will have an opportunity to experience foot-washing if they wish. Do not make it mandatory, but encourage each to participate. Begin by selecting several people and wash their feet and then ask them in turn to wash another's, and so on. You will need the following items:

- Two or three large bowls suitable for foot-washing
- Several pitchers of warm water
- Clean towels

In silence allow time for each to experience "foot-washing." Suggest they remain in prayer, asking that they give thought to the question, "Is there a person in your life who needs a gentle touch from you?"

As the washing of feet draws to a close, gather in a large circle, ask for prayer petitions, then close with the Lord's Prayer.

The Gift of Forgiveness

Scripture: Mt 26:69–75
Feast: Triduum
Music Suggestion: any selection from *Dream Journey*
    or "Without You, Lord"/*Gentle Sounds*

Most of us have made many mistakes in our lives. Sometimes, our mistakes seem so serious that we believe we can never be forgiven. We see no light at the end of the tunnel. We know within our hearts how badly we have messed up, even though it may not have been discovered yet. Our errors lie in silence within the caverns of our souls.

Take a moment and think of the men who surrounded Jesus. Do you think that one in particular really dropped the ball? (*Allow time for brief discussion.*) Judas, probably feeling that he could never be forgiven, hung himself. Only in the moment of death did he realize what he had done. But what about Peter? He climbed the mountaintop to see Elijah and Moses. Jesus called him Cephas, or the "rock" upon which he would build his church. Yet, in the hour of darkness Peter turned his face from our Lord. Was it fear? shame? Knowing our own pain when we know we have failed the test, do we have any concept of how Peter felt? The gift of forgiveness was within Peter's grasp; he only had to reach out of his shame and sorrow.

Let us release our imaginations to go back to the darkness of evening and the blackness of terror. This was a time of fear and betrayal, but it also was a time of forgiveness, offering us hope in the despair of our lives.

You may wish to introduce the following meditation by reading the first paragraph on page 70.

Meditation

Make yourself comfortable .... Close your eyes and shut out
the world around you .... Allow your arms to fall freely at your
side .... Relax in the calm .... Take a deep breath. Whisper
"Jesus" .... Let the breath out slowly, forming the words, "My
Savior" ....

You sit in silence around the long table .... Jesus passes the
cup to you and smiles sadly .... For this will be the end ....
Press the cup to your lips .... Smell the sweetness of the
grape.... Only James breaks the silence, "Join me now in
song. Let us raise our voices to our heavenly Father" .... The
song is sung, but there is no joy, no merrymaking. There is
only the silence of death's messenger .... Jesus sits on his
knees, raising his voice slightly, "This very night you will all fall
away because of me, for it is written: 'I will strike the
shepherd, and the sheep of the flock will be scattered'" ....
Your eyes meet Jesus'. You turn away in shame for all those
times you have forgotten his name .... Jesus places his hand
upon your shoulder—not to take away the pain, but to let you
know he feels your shame ....

Jesus stands, adjusting his robe, "After I have risen, I will go
ahead of you into Galilee" .... Peter rubs his scruffy beard and
quickly proclaims, "Even if all fall away on account of you, I
never will!" Only Peter can speak with such conviction ....
Jesus looks down at the floor, then speaks, "I will tell you the
truth, this very night before the rooster crows, you will disown
me three times" .... Peter makes a fist and slams the table ....
The cups dance on the uneven wood "Even if I am to die with
you, I will never disown you," he says, once again striking the
table .... All disciples say the same .... You nod your head in
agreement, looking downward ....

The meal is finished, the message delivered .... You make
your way down the dark stairway into the night .... No one
carries a lantern for fear of being seen .... Silently the group
follows Jesus to the Garden of Gethsemane .... The hour is
late and your eyes are filled with heaviness .... Although Jesus
has asked all of you to stay awake with him, the hour finds

you all fast asleep .... In the fog of slumber, Judas arrives ....
There is a large crowd with him, armed with swords and
clubs .... James huddles near you, whispering, "The chief
priests and elders have sent them to arrest Jesus. Truly, the
end is near!" .... Judas kisses Jesus' cheek and the night draws
to a close .... You quickly slide behind the large boulder where
a few moments before, Jesus knelt in prayer .... "What am I
expected to do?" you ask yourself ....

You rise from your hiding spot and follow the milling
crowd .... Jesus, his wrists wrapped with a leather thong,
stumbles through the night air .... Approaching a large house
sitting high above the city, Jesus is dragged to Caiaphas, the
high priest .... Teachers of the law and the elders are
assembled .... Sitting on carved wooden benches, they remind
you of our juries and courtrooms .... Look behind you .... It is
Peter. He walks among the guards, pulling his cloak tightly
around his head .... You find safety behind a group of
onlookers .... Fear grips your throat .... Weakness fills your
limbs .... The high priest bellows at Jesus, "Are you the
Christ, the Son of God?" .... Make your way through the
crowd, closer to Jesus .... Can you hear what he is saying to
the elders? (Pause briefly.)

Look around for Peter. Peter, the rock, the head of Christ's
church .... Peter sits in a crumpled heap in the courtyard ....
A servant girl passes by, asking, "You were with Jesus of
Galilee, were you not?" Peter turns his head away. "I don't
know what you are talking about" ....

Follow Peter to the gate .... Ask him what he is going to
do .... Before you can catch up with him, another girl cuts
across the dark courtyard, calling out to the guards, "This
fellow was with Jesus of Nazareth" .... Peter bustles past you
yelling, "I don't know what you are talking about!" .... A small
group of the curious block Peter's path .... Look directly at
Peter .... His eyes squint in the dark of night .... "You are one
of them!" the crowd rings out .... Peter squirms in denial, "For
the last time, I do not know this man!" ....

You go unnoticed .... Your silence rings loud in your ears ....
Immediately, in the distance, you hear a rooster crow ....
Peter, remembering Christ's words, falls to his knees .... Peter
reaches out for your hand and leads you to safety beyond the
gates .... He stops in the shadows, taking your face in his
rough calloused hands, speaking through his tears, "My friend,
how could I have turned away from Jesus?" .... You can feel
Peter's despair. In a choking voice, you ask, "Why did you do
this?" .... Hidden in the question is your own guilt for the
many times that you, too, have acted as though you did not
know him .... Peter wipes away the tears with the back of his
hand, "Talk costs nothing. I failed because I wasn't as strong
in the Lord as I thought. My faith disappeared" .... Peter
walks through the gates and into the night, not to gaze upon
his Lord again.

Jesus is allowed to sit, his head downcast as his judges mill
about the crowd .... One of them points to you, motioning for
you to join Jesus .... Jesus places his finger on his mouth,
"Shhhh!" for he fears for your safety .... Quietly, you make
your way to the side of Jesus .... He raises his hands, bloodied
from the tight ropes around his wrists, allowing them to come
to rest on your head, "You are forgiven, my child. God uses
even our failures for his good. Walk steady in your faith, for I
shall travel the road with you" .... His hands drop once again
to his lap. The pain of betrayal, the loneliness of death are
taking their toll ....

I will leave you alone with Jesus for the end of this long
night .... For tomorrow will bring both a closing and a
beginning. Take a few minutes to think of those times when
you have also hidden in the shadows of life .... The times
when you have failed .... Share these thoughts with the
Lord ....

Prayer

*Jesus, I come before you knowing the many times I
have failed. Grant that I may be strengthened by these
events. Use my failure to mold me into the person
that God wants me to become. Amen.*

It is time to take your leave of this sad night .... Jesus whispers, "I love you. For you these things will come to pass." Turn and walk into the night .... Open your eyes and return to this room.

Prayer Service

Supplies: petri dish, or large glass bowl for each group, small amount of sand or kitty litter, background music, paper and pencils

In small groups, join in a prayer service for each other in the name of Christ. Each person will be prayed with to overcome the feeling of pain or guilt. Invite the person to write down a time of guilt or pain on a slip of paper and symbolically fold the paper, placing it into the burning flame. The group will then lay hands on him or her in prayer or let the person know they care in some nonverbal way. As each group completes this celebration, close with one verse of "They Will Know We Are Christians by Our Love."

Forgive Them, Father

Scripture: Mk 15:21–40; Jn 19:1–30
Feast: Good Friday
Music Suggestion: any selection from *Thunderstorms* or *Dream Journey*, or "Without You, Lord"/*Gentle Sounds*

In Christian churches around the world, God's people gather to celebrate this holy day, Good Friday. There will not be a Mass on this day and services will close in prayerful silence. We are asked to walk through and to experience the death of our Lord, reflecting on the significance of his death within the framework of our own life.

When I relate the pain of Jesus, and the pain of his mother, Mary, I have to put it in my own perspective of agony. I, personally, only know of one pain that might compare. It brings my thoughts to the day our daughter died and upon learning of her death in a cold, sterile operating room, I let out a cry—a wild sound that came from deep within. There is no cry so deep, so devoid of hope, to compare. This in turn reminds me of the pain that God suffered on this day. He could have relieved his Son of this burden but chose instead to allow Christ's death to save all of mankind. Could any of us send our child to a painful death for any reason? I think not.

Most of us spend the rest of the church year thinking about anything and everything but this moment in time. We know about it but choose not to focus on it in a personal way. Let us close that gap by releasing our imaginations to travel to Golgotha and the day that changed our world forever.

You may wish to introduce the following meditation by reading the first paragraph on page 70.

Meditation

Find a comfortable position .... Close your eyes .... The
sounds of the day slowly drift beyond your hearing .... Feel
your limbs relax .... Move away in spirit from the people near
you .... Take a deep breath, whisper "Jesus" .... Let it out
slowly, whisper "my Savior" ....

It is early morning .... The night has been long .... You stand
on a rock-strewn hillside .... The cries of the dying fill the
air .... One by one, the bodies are removed from the
crosses .... The odor of death hangs heavy in the morning
sun .... Jesus is making his way up the path to his
own execution .... The crowd taunts Jesus with every final
step he takes .... Only his mother, Mary; Mary, his mother's
sister; and Mary of Magdala—along with John the
apostle—follow behind this parade of death .... Gone are the
other apostles and gone are the throngs that followed Jesus
for three years .... Shouting and jeers replace the cries of
adulation ....

Jesus stumbles and falls for the third time .... His legs are
bruised .... A crown of thorns is imbedded into his scalp ....
Blood pours down his anguished face mixing with sweat ....
His tattered garments are nearly gone, hanging loosely over
his shoulders. Only his cloak remains intact .... As he falls the
third time, his head turns toward you. His eyes dart through
the reality of pain. Lowering his eyes and raising up on one
knee, for a brief moment he looks directly into your eyes ....
He reaches toward you but the sting of a Roman whip slices
through the morning mist .... Jesus balances the 125-pound
crossbeam on his shoulder and attempts to rise under its
weight .... Simon of Cyrene, drafted into sharing the weight
of the beam, grimaces as the wood cuts into his shoulder .... It
is clear he does not want to share this burden with Jesus ....
Simon, noticing that the eyes of Jesus are cast upon you,
grunts, "Where were you when he needed help? He is your
friend, not mine!" (*Pause briefly.*)

Dirt from the rocky road and spittle from his enemies coat
Jesus' body and his clothing .... There is one other sound

carried on this morning's misery, the soft wails of suffering and loss ....

Women gather, unafraid to show their mourning .... Women who remember his words .... Women who danced at the wedding in Cana .... Women who watched as the daughter of a Roman soldier rose from her deathbed .... The women of Galilee weep tears of agony .... John attempts to comfort the mother of Jesus .... John and Mary pass by, almost within reach .... You can feel her anguish as her body convulses in pain .... At long last, Jesus reaches the top of the hillside .... It is almost over .... The crowd cackles in anger .... They push and shove to be in front .... Their thirst for blood betrays them ....

It is nearly noon .... The sun moves endlessly on, retracing its steps across the sky .... Clouds are dancing on the wind .... The heavy, rugged crossbeam is torn from Jesus' grasp and thrown upon the ground .... Jesus is offered wine drugged with bitter herbs to deaden the pain. He turns his head away .... The Roman captain of the guard shoves you out of the way .... Those of you who dare follow Jesus this far are tossed aside like fabric dolls .... Many in the crowd now hide from sight for fear of their own end ....

Jesus is thrown to the ground and placed upon the tree of death .... He lies motionless upon his cross, glancing to the heavens for the grace to die .... Soldiers stand guard, holding the crowd at a distance .... Two soldiers are each given large mallets of steel .... A discussion takes place between the captains and the men armed with the tools of suffering .... Not wanting Jesus to escape in the shroud of death too quickly, they decide to place the nails in his wrists to provide an anchor of sorts .... You shudder in sorrow .... You shudder in horror .... The first hammer is swung, hitting the nail sharply .... The loud sound of metal hitting metal echoes through the now-silent crowd .... Blood spurts into the air, a geyser of life, then falls sharply upon the ground, staining the soil with death .... A sharp crunching of bone crackles in your ears .... Over and over again, the soldier pounds the nails until at last the deed is accomplished .... Jesus bites into his lips in pain, looking to the heavens for release from his earthly body .... He gasps in pain as the cross is lifted upright, his full weight pulling on the nails .... He gasps once more; he can inhale but he cannot exhale with his arms outstretched .... A small sign is nailed to the cross, "The king of the Jews" ....

Mary lays her head upon John's shoulder, weeping. Her cries are muffled in the folds of John's cloak .... Roman soldiers kneel beneath the cross, gambling for the cape of Jesus .... Two robbers are also crucified on this morning, their crosses on either side of Jesus .... The crowd passes beneath the cross of Jesus, jeering and snarling, "If you are truly the Son of God come down from the cross and save yourself!" .... Look upward into his pain-contorted face, offering your love as the only solace. (*Pause briefly.*) A chief priest stands near the foot of the cross, taunting, "You are clever at saving others they say, but you can't even save yourself now!" .... The two robbers curse him .... You grab a sponge and dip it into a bucket and raise it upon the end of a stick, but Jesus knowing the end is near, turns his head away once again ....

Rays of sunlight warm the back of your neck and arms .... Suddenly, without warning, darkness covers the entire land .... There is a deep rumbling from the clouds .... The wind whistles through your hair .... It is noon, and death takes its last breath .... You fall back in fear for the heavens are bursting open with rain and wind .... For three hours you sat huddled near Mary, the mother of Jesus .... Mary, sensing your presence, calls out to you, "My child," she calls you by name, "he dies for you! He dies that you may have hope." .... Mary is not blaming you .... She is speaking the truth .... You fall to the ground beneath the cross in remorse for all the times you have turned your face away from his .... For the times your footsteps have taken you down the wrong path .... Your words remain unspoken .... Jesus, knowing your heart, nods. His head is upon his chest. He looks down on you and prays to his father, "Father, forgive them, they did not know what they were doing." The silence of remorse fills the air ....

Take this moment to talk with him before death covers the land. (*Pause.*)

Thunder shakes the earth .... The darkened sky is now devoid of light .... It is three o'clock in the afternoon .... For hours you have been a bystander of death .... Jesus calls out with a loud voice, "My God, my God, why have you deserted me?" .... At last, Jesus utters another loud cry, one from deep within .... A cry so loud and piercing that it could be that of an injured animal .... You will forever hear the sound .... It is the cry of death .... Jesus dismisses his spirit. Life has turned to death .... A Roman officer standing beneath the cross watches as Jesus dismisses his spirit, falling to his knees he calls out, "Truly, this is the Son of God!" .... Mary screams the cry of a mother .... A cry that signals death has taken her son, her baby ....

Prayer

Jesus, You alone are my Lord, my Messiah. Help me to see with your eyes, Lord, and to love with your heart. I fall to my knees before you for you have carried the burden of my sins to your cross. Forgive me, Lord. Amen.

The day has drawn to a close .... Mary sits at the base of the cross holding the body of her son .... She weeps in silence, rocking back and forth as she did so many years before, inviting peaceful slumber for her son .... John approaches you, wiping the tears from his cheeks, nodding toward Mary, he speaks, "The child in each of us always belongs to the mother." .... The words from a Christmas carol run through your mind—"What Child Is This?" .... His body, now lifeless, hangs like a limp doll in the arms of his mother .... Reach from the shadows and take his limp hand into yours .... Hold it for a moment .... There is no life within this body .... Warmth spreads through your being and you know this is a beginning, not an ending .... It is time now for you to take your leave .... Rise and walk away .... Open your eyes and return to this room.

Allow the group to sit in silence for a few minutes. Continue to keep the lights dim, play the background music. If using a selection from Thunderstorm, *you may want to replace it with a selection from* Dream Journey *or with "Without You, Lord"/*Gentle Sounds.

Prayer Service

Dim the lights. Place a cross, lit by candlelight or a small spotlight, in a place of honor and reverence. Continue the background music.

Read aloud Isaiah 53:2–6. Allow a few moments of silence. Invite those who wish to share their feelings. Stress that you want them to be honest and that there are no wrong answers. If the group needs more stimulus, ask each to share, "I feel _____ about the crucifixion of Jesus because _____."

At the close gather together in a circle, holding hands. Pray the Lord's Prayer. Dismiss quietly.

Be Opened!

Scripture: Mk 7:31–37
Feast: Ephphetha Rite or 23rd Sunday in Ordinary Time (B)
Music Suggestion: "When You Seek Me"/*Gentle Sounds*

The ephphetha rite or rite of opening the ears and mouth impresses upon us the need for grace that we may be able to *hear* the word of God and *profess* it to all who may hear for their salvation. Jesus knew that many would be deaf to the word of God, their ears deafened by the din of a fast-moving world. It is known as selective deafness.

Just as radio and television waves silently carry voices, sounds, and music once we turn them on, so it is with the word of God. Please join me in reliving the ephphetha rite as it was instituted by Jesus.

Meditation

Find a comfortable position .... Close your eyes .... Roll your shoulders .... Your arms and hands fall to a comfortable position .... Inhale the love of God .... Exhale, slowly .... Shut out the sounds and cares of the day .... Breathe deeply .... Exhale slowly .... Whisper "Jesus" ....

The sun dangles high above you in the heavens .... You have walked many miles across the hot desert sands .... Dirt lies in rivulets on your feet .... Sit down by the side of the road .... Take off your shoes .... Wipe away the sandy soil .... Sip upon the last water in your flask .... Moisten your lips .... Dust rises from a profusion of scuffling feet .... Travelers all—the old and bent, the young, the ill, and the lame, and the curious—join you in seeking the Lord .... Jesus awaits the masses on the shores of the Sea of Galilee ....

25. Be Opened!

Beyond the sloping hillside, the waters of the Sea of Galilee
rush to the waiting arms of land .... Walk down the path ....
Be careful not to slip .... At last, the cool water washes across
your feet .... Wade out a little farther .... Birds of the sea
herald the return of fishermen .... You feel a touch of a hand
upon your shoulder .... Turn and look .... It is your friend
Jesus .... He smiles. Leaning on your shoulder, he removes
his well-worn sandals .... Jesus dips his hand into the sea,
splashing the refreshing water on his face .... "Come, we must
go. The people need me," Jesus says somewhat wistfully ....
You walk arm in arm out of the water, along the shore, and
then up the sloping hillside ...

There is little shade .... Jesus works among the crowd .... The
blessings of God flow abundantly .... A small bevy of people
push through the masses, calling out, "Jesus, Jesus, cure this
man!" .... The curious crane their necks .... The faithful fall
into prayer .... A faceless women, shrouded in a dark blue veil
pushes the little man toward Jesus .... He trembles, falling
upon his knees at Jesus' feet .... Jesus looks with pity, a tear
dropping to his cheek .... The man speaks little, hears nothing
of the world .... The Lord takes him by the hand, leading him
to where you stand sweltering in the noonday sun ....

Jesus places his hand on the frail man's ears, then places his
fingers on his own tongue before touching the deaf man's
ears .... Jesus looks up to heaven and with a deep sigh, he
commands, "Ephphetha! Be opened!" .... The man's eyes fill
with tears of joy, turning his head to the right and to the left,
listening to the sounds of life for the first time .... The joyful
man bends at the waist, kissing the hand of Jesus, "Thank
you, Lord, truly you are the Son of God!" .... A rousing cheer
rings in your ears ....

Soon all have returned to their homes .... Only you and Jesus
remain .... Jesus looks tired but content .... The two of you
make your way down to the shore once again .... It is almost
evening .... The sun fades beyond the wall of the sea .... The
sea lies calm, patiently waiting for the cover of nightfall ....
"Come, my friend," Jesus beckons with his arm .... Sit next to

Jesus …. "Many know my name but do not know me. Many hear the word of God but do know the words …. They do not hear the love … the promise … the forgiveness …. How can they speak of God if they have not *heard* the word of God? ….

Taking your hands in his, Jesus basks in the quiet of evening …. "Soon you will make a commitment to my church. Come before this body with an open heart and ears ready to listen, lips ready to proclaim" …. Jesus touches first your right ear …. Then your left …. Then your closed lips with his thumb, "Ephphetha: that is, be opened, that you may profess the faith you hear, to the praise and glory of God" …. Raising his arms in prayer Jesus speaks to his Father, "Lord, I pray to you for this elect, who has now accepted the loving purpose and the mysteries that you revealed through me. As they profess their belief with their lips, may they have faith in their hearts and accomplish your will in their lives. I ask this of you, my Father in heaven" …. Jesus wraps his arms about you …. Drink in his love …. "What else may I do for you, my dear friend?" he asks …. Take a moment and talk to the Lord ….

Prayer

Father, through your holy prophets you proclaim to all who draw near you, "Wash and be cleaned," and through Christ you have granted us rebirth in the Spirit. Bless me, your servant, as I prepare for baptism. Fulfill your promise: sanctify me in preparation for your gifts, that I may come to be reborn as your child and enter the community of your Church. I ask this through Christ our Lord. Amen.

It is time for you to take your leave …. Jesus places his hand above your head offering his blessing, "May God be with you until we gather again to celebrate the paschal mystery" …. Once again he whispers a message meant only for you. (*Pause.*) Say good-bye for now …. Walk along the shore until it meets the roadway …. Open your eyes and return to this room.

Closing Prayer

Pray the Apostles' Creed in closing.

Maintain a quiet atmosphere. If the elect are to leave the premises, ask that they do so in silence, without speaking.

In the Beginning

Scripture: Gen 1:1–2:2 (Easter Vigil Reading 1)

This will be a group reading with all joining in on the response: "Then God said, 'This is good!'" Select three readers, each reading one paragraph, then rotating in sequence. Pause for the group response following each reading.

Suggestion: Ask the group to begin their response with a whisper, gradually raising their voices with each response. Final response should be a rousing shout.

The Wonders of God— A Walk of Praise and Thanksgiving:

Allow twenty minutes to walk outside in silence. (If weather makes the walk outside impossible, ask them to remain in silence meditating on an imaginary walk through the woods, or a day at the shore; a place they would most want to be.)

Invite them to find something in nature that most reminds them of their own walk with the Lord (perhaps a seedling, or seed pod, or jagged rock that has yet to have its surface smoothed by time and experience). They may want to bring this item back with them to share with the group. When the group returns, you may find it helpful to start the sharing.

Faith in the Face
Of Death

Scripture: Gen 22:1–18 (Easter Vigil Reading 2); Mk 14:22–23
Music Suggestion: any selection from *The Sea*
or "When You Seek Me"/*Gentle Sounds*

After waiting a lifetime, Sarah and Abraham finally became parents. In Sarah's old age, God bestowed the miracle of life. Abraham adored his son, just as we love our children. God put Abraham to a true test of faith. Without striking any bargains or arguing, he accepted the will of God for him. He passed the test.

Can we?

God's favored son, Abraham, is asked to move in faith—the ultimate faith—to answer God's call. Soon after reading this passage some years ago, I found myself questioning the strength of my own faith in God. He gives and gives, loves, and forgives, and yet we question when we are asked to respond ourselves. Eighteen months earlier our youngest daughter had died in the sterile atmosphere of an operating room. Now, I found myself looking at the greatest gift of God, our new daughter—sweet and pink, happy and warm, a laughing, happy child of God. I knew that I would never have the faith of Abraham. However, once again God replied to my unspoken words, "I will not test you beyond your ability to respond in faith." My Lord, my God, knew my heart.

You may wish to invite a parish leader to give a short talk on his or her own answer to the Lord's call to move in faith. "Do you trust me?" our Lord asks. The talk should be no longer than five to ten minutes.

I have chosen to use the following passage from the New Testament rather than Genesis 22:1–18. I believe that Peter's step of faith would offer better comparisons to our lives today.

Within the pages of the New Testament we find that God, through his Son, Jesus, once again asks his chosen child—this time, Peter—to reach out in faith. Jesus awaits our answer. He calls our name from the depths of our despair. He offers his hand to steady and guide us—and yet, so often, we are deaf to his call and blind to his understanding of our human nature. In times of moral or physical danger, it often becomes difficult to reach out in absolute faith.

Meditation

Let us spend a few moments together in prayer and meditation, separate as individuals, united in the body of Christ. We are on the shore of the Sea of Galilee. The water is surrounded by hills. The wind whips around the base of the hillsides, each pass picking up in speed. Small craft often find themselves in danger quickly.

Find a comfortable position .... Close your eyes .... Allow the cares of the day to drift from view .... Shrug your shoulders, releasing the tensions of the day .... Take a deep breath .... As you draw in your breath, whisper "Jesus" .... Exhale slowly; whisper "My Lord."

You are seated on the sandy shore of the Sea of Galilee .... Water pushes onto the land, then races back into the sea, leaving damp prints on the muddy shore .... Early evening whispers its shadows across the sea .... Lake waters lap at the shore .... Several small boats prepare to cast off .... Peter moves about the deck of his boat, allowing the soft winds to pull through his snarled red hair .... Peter calls out, "Ready to go!" .... Jesus climbs the rope ladder to the edge of the deck, looks up, and recognizes you .... He calls your name, "Would you like to come with us?" .... Run down to the water's edge .... Your feet sink in the muddy mire ....

27. Faith in the Face of Death

Jesus looking tired and gaunt, takes a seat on the wooden deck, then moves over, making room for you .... He instructs the men to row to the opposite side of the lake, away from the crowds. This will be a time of prayer for Jesus. A time with his Father, God .... Moonlight streaks the water with its yellow haze, offering a sense of direction through the night .... Reaching the shore, a large purple mountain rises above the water, casting its dark shadow over the boat and the sea .... Jesus steps out of the boat, waves good-bye, and instructs the disciples to come back for him.

As the boat leaves Jesus and the shore behind, you feel the gentle rolling of the waves beneath the boat .... In the glow of the moonlight, the mountain's shadow grows smaller .... Time passes quickly amid the soft murmuring of the disciples' voices; it is time to return for Jesus .... The air stirs around you, whipping the sea into frothy white foam .... Peter's hands grip the wheel, his knuckles white .... Peter shouts, "The winds are pushing us farther out! We surely will not be able to reach Jesus" .... John hands you an oar, "Row with all your might!" .... Splinters of wood dig into your hands as you pull against the force of the sea .... The boat does not respond to the failing oars .... A low, roaring rumble echoes against the hills .... Darkness begins to cover the sea .... Windswept waves wash over the deck ....

In the direction of the distant shore, a strange figure appears above the lake .... It moves slowly, on top of the water, inching its way toward the boat .... The disciples cry out, "It's a ghost!" .... You peek over the railing, afraid to see and afraid not to see .... From the shifting water and the fog-shrouded lake you hear, "Do not be afraid! It is I, Jesus!" .... The ghostly figure glides through the foamy sea .... Peer into the fog .... It is Jesus! .... The skeptics take turns calling out, "Who are you?" .... Peter, always brave, always the first to speak, demands, "If that is you, Lord, tell me to come to you on the water" .... You wonder how seriously Peter must take himself ....

Beyond the fog, beyond the cold spray of water, the soft voice of Jesus awakens the night air, "Peter, come to me!" .... Peter hesitates, looking first at the other men, no doubt debating what will look the least ridiculous, then slowly climbs out of the boat on uncertain legs into the cold, dark waters .... Waves and wind pound the boat .... Peter immediately begins to sink .... Winds of doubt howl .... "I am afraid! Help me, Lord!" Peter cries in fear .... Jesus reaches out his hand to Peter, "Oh, you of little faith—why do you doubt me?" .... Jesus holds Peter's hand in his. Peter rises to rest upon the sea ....

They walk, hand in hand, toward the small craft .... Suddenly, Jesus stops, resting on the crest of a wave .... Peter stammers, once again in fear .... Jesus calls your name—not James's or John's, but your name .... "Step out of the boat. Come to me, my friend" .... I will leave you alone to decide if you are going to step out of the boat onto the bubbling sea of life .... Tell Jesus how you feel. (*Pause.*)

The waters are stilled .... The night is clouded now with silence .... You are only aware of your own heartbeat .... Jesus speaks for all to hear, "May God's blessings be with you of faith" ....

You and Jesus settle back against the bow of the boat once again. Peter stands at the wheel, mumbling to himself .... Jesus turns to you, "Asking you to get out of the boat was a test, you know? This test will be the first of many. Your life is a journey of faith. If you could measure your faith, is there enough? Will you walk with me?" (*Pause until they grow restless.*)

Prayer

Jesus, I, like Abraham and Peter, accept the test of my own faith. There are fears that come in the dark of life and I forget to reach out in trust. Fill me with the strength of your faith. Steady my walk with you. Bond this community in your love. Amen.

It is time to return to shore and say good-bye to Jesus .... Step out of the boat .... Walk up the sandy path .... Turn and wave once more .... Open your eyes and return to this room.

Discussion

In small groups share the answer to the following questions:

- Is Jesus inviting you to "get out of the boat" in some area of your life?
- Are you prepared to answer Jesus' call of faith?
- Has there been a time in your life when you felt the presence of Jesus influencing your actions ?

Step into the Light

Scripture: Ex 14:15–15:1 (Easter Vigil Reading 3)

> *Then the Lord said to Moses, "... Use your rod—hold it out over the water, and the sea will open up a path before you, and all the people of Israel shall walk through on dry ground!" (Ex 14:15–16).*

Supplies: old magazines, newspaper, glue or tape, paper lunch bags, scissors

As we venture onward on our journey of faith, God continues to work miracles for each of us, protecting and guiding us on our pathway to God. Problems for the Israelites were not simple nor is our life without pain and suffering.

Activity

Create a paper-sack collage out of newspaper and magazine tear-outs. Allow ten minutes to prepare the bags. Then break into small groups, each person explaining first the outside of their bag; then go around the second time, each explaining the inside of the bag.

- *Outside:* Select tear-outs that depict the way you were before you started the catechumenate process.
- *Inside:* Select tear-outs that depict the way you are now, or the way you hope to be.

Suggestion: This may be a good time to invite a member of the RCIA team to briefly (five minutes) share what God has done for them during this catechumenate process.

A Love Letter

Scripture: Isa 54:5–14 (Easter Vigil Reading 4)

> *For the mountains may depart and the hills disappear, but my kindness shall not leave you. My promise of peace for you will never be broken, says the Lord who has mercy upon you (Isa 54:10).*

Supplies: Bibles or copies of Isaiah 54:4–10, a candle, background music of choice

God speaks to us through the words of the prophet Isaiah. Isaiah brings the poetry of God's love to the people of Jerusalem, a love letter from God to his people. In this reading, it is good to remember that God speaks to us as a lover. God seeks to be reconciled with us and to share his grace and love with us. Read these words of love as you walk alone outdoors, or sit quietly, allowing your thoughts to form a picture of God that is as close as your outstretched hand. Speak to him with your soul. Allow God to lavish you with his love. Drink in his praises, for you are his beloved.

Darken the room. Light one candle; play background music.

Prayer Litany

Following the silent time, gather together to offer petitions.

Response: Lord, hear our prayer.

Leader: Guide us, Lord, in our journey of faith

Response

Leader: Stand beside us in all that we do …

Response

Leader: Strengthen us to live in your image ...

Response

Leader: Enrich our faith in you, now and forever ...

Response

Leader: Forgive our sins and trespasses

Response

Leader: Fill us with your love ...

Response

Close this segment by praying the Apostles' Creed.

Come and Have New Life

Scripture: Isa 55:1–11 (Easter Vigil Reading 5)

> *Come and have new life as the heavens
> scatter snow and rain upon the ground to
> water the earth, thus causing fields of grain to
> thrive, yielding bread for the farmer and food
> for the hungry.*
>
> *So also is my word. My word always bears
> fruit. It shall accomplish all I want it to, and
> prosper everywhere I send it (Isa 55:10–11).*

This passage speaks to us concerning the power of the Word of God.

Recently, during a week-long retreat, my spiritual director gave me a reading to meditate on (Exodus 3:2–5). I was given instructions to read and then read again, over and over, until I heard the message that was for me. I did not fully grasp its meaning nor its connection to me. In fact, it was several days before my mind, or perhaps my own spirit, would allow me to understand what God was saying to me.

Now I ask you to read Isaiah 55:1–11 several times. Repeat the verse. Listen for what God is saying to you. Meditate on these words. The Word of God has set forth rules to live by, a road map to God and God's kingdom. In this reading from Isaiah, our God offers an invitation to each of us, "Come to the water. Come and be refreshed. Come and have a new life." Do you hear his voice?

At the designated time, return to this room. If the Spirit leads you, please share your encounter with the Word of the Lord with the group. *(Allow fifteen minutes.)*

- What part of the reading spoke to your heart?
- How has the Word of God influenced the changes in your life?

Springs of Salvation

Scripture: Isa 12:2–3,4,5–6 (Easter Vigil Response to Reading 5)

Prayer

Response: You will draw water joyfully from the springs of salvation.

Leader: God indeed is my savior;
      I am confident and unafraid.
      My strength and my courage is the Lord,
      and he has been my savior.
      With joy you will draw water
      at the fountain of salvation.

Response

Leader: Give thanks to the Lord, acclaim his name;
      among the nations make known his deeds,
      proclaim how exalted is his name.

Response

Leader: Sing praise to the Lord for his glorious
      achievement;
      let this be known throughout the earth.
      Shout with exultation, O city of Zion,
      for great in your midst
      is the Holy One of Israel!

Response

Pleasing Father God

Scripture: Bar 3:9–15,32—4:4 (Easter Vigil Reading 6)

> *Happy are we, O Israel,*
> *for we know what is pleasing to*
> *God (Bar 4:4).*

The world bangs on our ears and on our intellect with the modern version of wisdom: "Vote for him/her." "The wise decision would be to ...." "Parents should ...." On and on, it always assaults our lifestyles. Does the wisdom of the world meet the standards of God?

Within your small groups, take a few moments for each person to share his/her answer to the first question and insights, then continue on to the second question:

- Do you seek to please God or do you seek rave reviews from your fellow beings?
- Has this changed since beginning the catechumenate journey?

As a group give thought to examples of the world's advice for seeking prosperity and happiness. Using Scripture, compare what you feel God's response would be to the first list. If there is time, you may want to share these contradictory views with the whole group.

A New Heart, A New Spirit

Scripture: Ezek 36:16–17,18–28 (Easter Vigil Reading 7)

> *I will sprinkle clean water upon you, and you
> shall be clean from all your uncleannesses,
> and from all your idols I will cleanse you. A
> new heart I will give you, and a new spirit I
> will put within you; and I will remove from
> your body the heart of stone and give you a
> heart of flesh (Ezek 36:25–26).*

Through the pages of time, Ezekiel brought us God's Good
News: Through the grace received in reception of the
sacraments, God has promised that we shall walk on this earth
anew. Our hearts and our spirits shall be raised from the
depths of sin to new creation. Thank you, Lord.

Along our journey of faith we have made changes in our life,
and our points of view. We stand together as new creations
before humans and God!

The reception of this gift also means change and change can
be a fearful process.

Quiet Time

*Allow fifteen minutes for the group to meditate in silence
on the following questions:*

- What changes do you feel God is asking of you and how
  will they affect your life and the lives of those around you?
- What will you ask of God in this "new creation"?

137

It may be helpful to have them jot these thoughts down in their journals.

Optional Activity: Pass the Coat

Allow a few moments for the group to meditate on the reading and the new creation of their hearts. Ask them to reflect on the changes that may need to be made and what they would ask of God in this "new creation."

Give each small group a heavy coat. In silence, ask one person to use the coat to depict the changes they would like to see take place in the new creation of their heart and spirit. Then, without comment, pass the coat to the next person, until everyone has treated the coat according to what he/she would want to happen during this retreat. Then pass the coat around a second time and let each one explain what he/she did. This whole activity should take about fifteen minutes.

Live in The Newness of Life

Scripture: Rom 6:3–11 (Easter Vigil Epistle Reading)

> *Therefore we have been buried with him by baptism into death, so that, just as Christ was raised from the dead by the glory of the Father, we too might walk in newness of life (Rom 6:4).*

Suggestion: This would be an excellent opportunity to invite someone who went through the catechumenate program recently to give a short talk on his/her journey of faith. Discuss the changes that have come about in his/her life. The talk should respond to the fears that he/she may have had before reception of the sacraments and the hope that he/she now carries. Allow for questions and answers. (Ten minutes.)

- Invite a godparent/sponsor to share how being a sponsor/godparent has made a difference in his/her own life. (Five minutes.)

- Invite the elect to respond to the following question: Has there been a time during Lent that was particularly meaningful for you, an experience in which you were touched deeply? Was there a time or moment when you were consciously aware of the presence of God? When?

Prayer Service

Supplies: bowls of water, towels, a candle, a crucifix, background music

You may want to move outdoors for this prayer service. Place a large bowl of water, a crucifix, and a candle together. Ask each person to come forward, and dipping his/her hands into the water with fists clenched, indicating how he/she first came to the group. Then ask the person gradually to open his/her hands, feeling the freedom of walking with our Lord. Ask members of the team to dry the person's hands, in silence. Invite them to repeat, "I live in the newness of life," as their hands are dried.

He Is Risen!

Scripture Reading: Mt 28:1–10; Mk 16:1–7; Lk 24:1–12
    (Easter Vigil Gospel Readings)
Music Suggestion: "We Believe in You"/*Gentle Sounds*
    or "Only a Shadow"/*Gentle Sounds*

> " ... you are looking for Jesus of Nazareth,
> who was crucified. He has been raised; he is
> not here." (Mk 16:6).

This final Scripture would best be experienced in a church or a
chapel. If this is not available, select a quiet room that has not
been used as yet for this retreat. Dim the lights. If possible,
open the doors of an empty tabernacle in a place of honor or
a wooden cross (not a crucifix). If using a cross, place the light
in front of it in order to cast a shadow. Gather the elect in a
circle surrounding the empty tabernacle or cross. Provide floor
pillows and space to find a comfortable position for the
meditation.

A few weeks ago we embarked on yet another road on our
journey of faith—Lent. Soon, Christ's promise of resurrection
will become a reality for each of us. We now find ourselves
gathered around an open tabernacle, the doors open,
standing at attention, guarding the emptiness of space.
(*Or a barren cross, a symbol of Christ's death, a symbol of
his life.*)

The resurrection of Jesus challenges our faith and our
imagination and our ability to explain it to nonbelievers. Why
should we not feel stunned to find the tomb empty? The
disciples lived with our Lord, they experienced miracle after
miracle, and yet they were stunned. Some refused to believe

without proof. On the morning of the third day following the death of Jesus, the reign of God had arrived.

Let us relive that morning within the pages of our imaginations.

Meditation

Make yourself comfortable .... Close your eyes .... Shut out the world around you .... Feel your body relax .... Take a deep breath .... Let it out slowly .... Whisper "Jesus" ....

It is early morning; the sun is reluctant to take on the day .... Your Lord was swept into the arms of death but three days ago .... The ones who called you "friend" are no longer in sight .... Fear has driven them into the shadows .... The women who followed Jesus from Galilee make their way through the mist to anoint his body with oils .... Mary of Magdala, her long dark hair blowing in the gentle winds of spring, invites you to join them in this pilgrimage of service .... Grab a jacket. The morning air is chilly and damp .... Mary hands you a bottle of oil .... One of the women asks, "Who will move the big stone away from the entrance to the tomb so that we can go inside?" .... One of the women, as yet unknown to you, shrugs her shoulders and points a finger in your direction ....

The rock-strewn hillside is barren except for low-lying brush .... Rocks cut into your sandal-clad feet .... Winds whistle through your hair and chill your hands .... The hillside seemingly steps aside, exposing rays of sunlight .... With the presence of light comes a new radiance .... Clouds of darkness and the shadow of death are lifted .... Flowers now adorn the path .... White lilies wave in the breeze .... Butterflies flit from flower to flower .... As you reach the crest of the hill, glance to your right .... There is the tomb of Jesus! .... The doorway of the tomb is rolled away. "Who has done this?" asks an older woman .... Mary nudges you forward, but you do not want to go .... "Come on, let's look!" she suggests .... Curiosity has momentarily replaced sorrow .... You take one cautious step at a time until you reach the doorway .... Fear grips your stomach and you turn away .... Persistently, Mary

makes sure you do not waiver .... The other women stand
huddled in shock, whispering in fear .... Forced to peer inside
the tomb, you jolt in fear .... "It is empty!" .... You crouch
into the tomb, demanding a candle, for who knows what is
hiding in the shadows of death .... Strips of white woven cloth
lie scattered at your feet .... There is a stirring from the
doorway of the tomb .... A bright light dazzles your eyes .... A
young man, dressed entirely in white, speaks to you. "Why are
you looking in a tomb for someone who is alive? He is not
here! Jesus is not dead" .... The angel slowly rises to his
feet .... "Remember, he told you that he would be handed
over to people who would crucify him but on the third day
would rise from the dead. My friends, Jesus has been raised
up" .... Your heart pounds, for perhaps only you know what
has happened on this day .... Mary begins to cry, insisting the
body of Jesus has been stolen .... Reach out to her ....

Three of the women run off down the path toward
Jerusalem .... Dust flies from their feet .... "They will tell
everyone that the body of Jesus has disappeared," Mary
explains .... Together you walk over to a large olive tree ....
You sit beneath its huge branches .... Mary cries softly ....
Though you know what to expect, your spirit is uneasy ....
Wiping the tears from her cheek, she draws in her breath in
fear .... You turn quickly .... A slender man stands at her
side .... The man's forehead wrinkles .... He places a
calloused hand on your shoulder .... You are no longer
afraid .... In a soft, unfamiliar voice, he asks, "Who are you
looking for?" .... Mary pulls her shawl around her shoulders as
a shield from the unknown. "Where is Jesus?" she
demands .... Gently, the stranger grasps Mary's hand,
whispering, "Mary!" over and over .... Mary once again wipes
the tears from her eyes and then stares intently at the man ....
She lets out a gasp, "It is Jesus!" .... The appearance of the
curious man, so totally familiar and yet unknown to you,
quickens your heartbeat .... He looks at you, smiling slightly,
your name is upon his lips .... "Did you also think that I
abandoned you? My friend, what God has done for me, he will
do for you. I have chosen you to carry my message to

others" .... "Why me?" you stutter, your mind swirling with questions and uncertainty .... Shadows of the days in your past cross your mind .... Jesus, your Lord, your God, smiles faintly, "Do not go there, my child, I am with you today," he whispers .... You step forward into his open arms .... Jesus is alive!

The soft blades of grass on the hilltop are tousled by the breeze. New blossoms burst through petals of green .... Breathe in the sweet fragrance of the flowers .... Mary gathers the other women about her, talking excitedly .... She runs down the hill to tell others about the appearance of Jesus .... Jesus *is* alive!

You stand alone with Jesus in this beautiful place .... Rays of sun warm the chill of the new day .... Jesus holds out his loving arms to you once again .... Feel his arms wrap around you, holding you secure in his love .... He speaks now only to you, "I will always keep my promises to you, my child." Cradling your face in his hands, he looks deep into your eyes, beyond today, perhaps beyond tomorrow .... At last he speaks, "There have been times when you have doubted my presence in your life. I have walked your walk waiting for this day. You are my beloved," he whispers .... Imagine that you are very small .... Climb up onto his lap .... Feel his love and protection. Take this time to talk to Jesus .... Speak to him from your heart, listen with your spirit .... I will leave you alone with Jesus ....

Prayer

Dearest Jesus, through my imagination I witnessed the events of Easter morning. Through you, I, too, will experience life everlasting. May I live with this hope in the time to come. May your Spirit strengthen me in times of weakness and in trials. May my life give witness to the world of all that you are and will be. Amen.

Prayer Service

The lights should remain low, using only candlelight. Prepare a table for an agape with bread and wine.

Gather in a circle of hope and peace. Sing a familiar song of celebration. Then ask each person to come forward to the table, breaking off a piece of bread, taking a sip of the wine or grape juice, and repeating the acclamation, "Jesus is with us!"

Anyone who wishes may share his/her thoughts with the group at this time.

Following the resurrection, Jesus greeted his friends with, "Peace, my friends." Let us close by sharing this sign of peace with each other.

Part 4

*Period Of
Postbaptismal
Catechesis
Or Mystagogy*

Your Touch Is Enough; I Believe!

Scripture: Jn 20:19–31
Feast: 2nd Sunday of Easter (ABC)
Music Suggestion: any selection from *Dream Journey*
    or "When You Seek Me"/*Gentle Sounds*

Faith is a gift from God. It is not something that you can analyze or just hope for. Faith comes when we still believe in the glory of our Lord, even though we don't know all the answers. This belief thrusts us into a lifelong relationship with God. Doubts will come and go; faith will sustain us. Keep in mind that Jesus never turned away from Peter, despite his lack of faith or courage. He did not send his doubting apostles away because they didn't understand the significance of the time they spend with our Lord. Does this not give you hope?

If Jesus walked into this room, what would it take for you to believe? Would one touch be enough for you? During the ministry of Jesus, people would often reach out to touch Jesus; it was a touch that they would always remember. It was a touch so filled with love they could feel it flow through their bodies. It was a touch that would last a lifetime.

In this day we cannot reach out and touch Jesus with our hands, but we can always feel the presence of him. Thomas, a faithful apostle, had a hard time believing at times. He demanded proof: to touch the wounds of his Lord. Using our imaginations, let's relive this special moment in time. It is Easter Sunday evening. You are one of the disciples. Will one touch be enough for you to believe?

Meditation

Close your eyes .... Stretch out your arms .... Allow them to go limp, falling to a comfortable position .... Relax .... Let the cares and sounds of the day fade away .... Take a deep breath .... Let it out slowly .... Whisper "Jesus" ....

One by one the disciples have crept into the doorway of an old dilapidated building standing on the edge of the city .... You have found your way through the night's shadows .... Slowly ease yourself up the wooden stairway, moving in silence .... Creak! groans the decaying step .... A chill moves through you .... Ssshhh! .... You feel your heart pounding against your chest .... Roman soldiers cover the street like the web of a spider .... You never know where they will be until it is too late .... They are looking for Jesus' followers .... They search every nook and cranny of every building, and every dark street ....

You are now stepping into a darkened room at the top of the stairs .... Peter moves over to the door, pulling the lock shut .... James closes the window shutters, shutting out the last glimmer of light .... You hold a candle in your shaking hands, afraid to light its wick .... The room is crowded and warm .... People speak in whispers .... You hear a woman sobbing .... A voice from the darkness speaks, "The tomb was empty!" ....

You huddle in the shadows, feeling alone .... Suddenly, Jesus is standing in front of you .... Can you see him? .... "Peace, my friend," he whispers .... Jesus knows that you are startled .... He reaches out to comfort you .... His hand almost touches yours, then pulls back, turning his palms upward .... His hands move to his torso, then pulling his garment loose he shows you the wound on his side—a slice of flesh still dangles free from the gash .... Jesus looks directly at you now, the light from a small candle flickering across his face .... "Do you believe?" he asks .... Take time to answer his question. (*Pause for a moment.*) Peter grumbles over the absence of Thomas, for all must know of the return of Jesus.

149

Later the same evening you walk with a few disciples to
Thomas's home, crouching in the arms of shadows .... The
disciples tell Thomas what they have seen .... Thomas, young
and straight, but stubborn, shakes his head in disbelief .... Tell
him what you have seen this day .... Thomas turns his back
and walks away from you. "I'll believe when I can touch the
hands of Jesus myself, and put my hand into the gash in his
side" .... Words truly fall upon deaf ears. He leaves in
disbelief ....

One week has gone by .... You once again find yourself in the
small upstairs room .... Thomas, your friend, sits close by your
side in the haze of darkness .... Clatter! .... Crash! .... The
footsteps of Roman soldiers in the street below echo through
the night .... Fear tickles your spine .... Grab for Thomas's
hand .... The candle flickers, nearly dying away .... Voices are
stilled .... Hear the quiet .... You feel a presence beside
you .... It is Jesus! .... "Peace, my friends. Do not be afraid,"
he commands .... You are no longer afraid .... Nothing can
harm you, no enemy can destroy you. Jesus stands before all
who have gathered in this place ....

Jesus turns to Thomas. "Touch the marks on my hands, feel
the wound in my side" .... Thomas slowly reaches forward,
barely making contact with Jesus' hands .... "My Lord, my
God!" exclaims Thomas, falling to his knees .... Jesus bends
low, helping Thomas to his feet. "Thomas, you believed
because you have seen, but blessed are people who believe but
have not seen" ....

The followers gather around Jesus, some embracing, some
not daring to touch him. At last, the others mill about the
room, talking about the events of tonight .... This time will
always be with you .... From the shadows Jesus takes your
hand into his .... Hold it tightly .... Can you feel his touch? ....
Feel the warmth of his hand .... You feel love .... You feel
truth .... You feel faith ....

Jesus looks beyond your being, asking, "In the days to come,
you may feel doubt. Do not despair, for it is normal to
question from time to time .... If others grow to doubt your

faith because of your actions, this is not good. Always be my witness. Do you believe, my friend?" .... I will leave you alone with Jesus to answer this question.

Prayer

Jesus, I want to believe in you. I need to believe in you to provide the strength in my life. I do believe in you. May your Holy Spirit calm and fill me, all the days of my life. May my journey of faith be witness to your life. Amen.

Jesus is once again surrounded by his friends .... Reaching out across the crowd, he places a hand on your shoulder .... Turn and walk down the narrow stairway out into the streets below .... Open your eyes and return to this room.

Discussion

If you have a large group of neophytes, you may wish to break down into several smaller groups. Open sharing on the following questions is desirable.

- Complete this sentence, "If I were Thomas and this happened to me, I would feel ...
- Was there a high point for you during the Easter vigil? Why was this significant for you?
- Did you experience the presence of God? Explain.
- What are your hopes now?
- What are your fears?
- How can you feel the presence of Jesus in your world?

Closing Prayer

Read 1 Peter 1:8–9.

Response: We believe in you, Lord Jesus Christ.

Please invite the neophytes to participate in a litany of thanksgiving. They are to complete the following sentence in their own words and be prepared to offer their own prayer of thanksgiving: The Lord has risen! I rejoice and give thanks for ...

Leader: We give thanks for all of the signs of your love for us. We offer thanks for each of the neophytes (*name*). Through these children of God, the Church has experienced a renewal of our life in Christ.

We now ask that they offer their own words of praise and thanksgiving.

Response: The Lord has risen! I rejoice and give thanks for ...

Conclude by offering a sign of peace.

A Walk in Faith

Scripture: Lk 24:13–31
Feast: 3rd Sunday of Easter (A)
Music Suggestion: "When You Seek Me"/*Gentle Sounds*

We now find ourselves on the tough part of our faith journey—living it day in and day out. Most of us wonder what we could contribute to building the kingdom when we are fighting for our own foothold in faith. Our stories are told within the pages of Exodus, for we, too, are a people on a pilgrimage. Our mission is great; at times our attempts to implement it are less than perfect.

As a member of the laity of our Church, you are the power switch. Work is accomplished, goals are set, action is taken because of you. Have you realized that you are tremendously important to God's plan for the world? Do you wonder if the Holy Spirit forgot about you? Well, he didn't. Once you were baptized, you became a part of the priesthood of the faithful, called on to help build God's kingdom. Where does a job of this importance begin? Build the kingdom of God from within the walls of your own home. It will soon spill over to all that you do and say.

Were the goals of the apostles clear-cut? Did they just move ahead with "the plan"? More than likely, they were far less sure of the events of the day than you will ever be. Jesus knew they failed to understand his death, let alone his resurrection. He promised them that he would never leave them alone. Taken at face value, their hope soon faded with the death of Jesus. They felt abandoned and alone. Although the tomb was found empty on Sunday morning and some even said they saw Jesus, this failed to impress most of his followers. Two of his friends, including Cleopas gave up on seeing Jesus again and decided to return to their homes in Emmaus. These two men had a surprise coming! Jesus never forgets his friends or his promises to them.

Let's release our imaginations and travel back to a warm spring day and see what happens on their journey of faith.

Meditation

Find a comfortable position .... Close your eyes .... Shrug your shoulders, releasing the cares of the day .... Take a deep breath .... Let it out slowly, whisper "Jesus" ....

The noonday sun finds you on the road to Emmaus. The events of the past three days rest heavily upon your mind. What was real and what was not? repeats over and over .... The dirt from the roadway cakes your feet in clouds of sand .... Your shoulders sag in despair .... Jesus is gone forever .... Ahead of you, in the glare of the sun, there are two men .... You have seen them with Jesus before .... Look closely .... You recognize one of the men, Cleopas .... Call out to him ....

Cleopas, his shoulders rolled inward, greets you with a warm hug. His friend, a tall man with dark hair, shakes your hand .... Cleopas explains that they are returning to their homes in Emmaus now that Jesus is gone .... You feel their sadness; for you too shall miss him .... The pace of the walk slows as the two men speak of their loneliness and the death of Jesus .... The loss of your friend stings your eyes, sending tears down your cheeks ....

Turning a bend in the road, another man joins your group .... He turns to you, asking, "What are you talking about?" .... "Haven't you heard what happened?" interrupts Cleopas. "Our Master, Jesus, died on a cross. He was buried three days ago. It is told by the women who went to anoint his body that the tomb was empty. He promised that he would never leave us—now look at us!" .... Embarrassed by the coarseness of Cleopas, you attempt to tell the stranger what you know of Jesus. (*Pause.*) The gentle man listens intently, an occasional

154

smile crosses his lips, then fades away. "Is this why you seem
so sad?" he asks .... The stranger offers you his hand .... His
grip is warm and tender .... As you continue your journey
toward Emmaus, the stranger begins to speak to you about
the glory of God and things in Scripture concerning the
Messiah .... Cleopas interrupts, "But why did Jesus die?" ....
The man turns to Cleopas and his friend, "You really don't
know very much. Jesus died in order to bring new life to the
people. I know that you have heard this before" .... The words
ring in your ears with a familiar melody .... You question
silently ....

The day is spent and the sun begins to settle behind the
rooftops .... You are know standing in front of Cleopas'
house .... The walls are made of bricks of mud. A flat roof
surrounds the courtyard .... The man shakes hands with your
friends, offering his good-byes .... Cleopas then invites the
stranger to supper .... You walk through the doorway to the
house, making your way to the kitchen area .... Light a lamp
and clear off the table .... Look through the cupboards
hurriedly .... On a long wooden table you place bowls
containing a few dried fish, and fruit and nuts .... There is also
a loaf of fresh bread and some wine ....

Cleopas and his friend take their places at the table .... The
guest invites you to sit beside him, patting the floor pillows ....
Cleopas light the table candle and offers thanks to God for the
food .... The visitor smiles warmly .... "Tell us more stories
from Scripture," Cleopas begs .... The man tells stories of
Noah and Jonah, wonderful stories about the kingdom of
God .... Pass the basket of warm bread .... The stranger
receives the bread from your hands, blesses it and hands you a
piece first .... Place the bread upon your tongue .... Next, he
hands the bread to the two men across the table .... Your
mouth drops open in disbelief .... This is Jesus! .... It is not
the familiar face nor his speech, but Jesus is with you now in
another form .... You have recognized Jesus in the breaking
of the bread, a sign of unity with him .... Your friends babble
with excitement for they too have recognized Jesus ....

Jesus takes your hand in his, leading you out into the garden ....' The evening air carries the sweet fragrance of rose blossoms .... You are alone with Jesus .... He leans forward, whispering, "I will never leave you." Jesus folds one arm around you, holding you close to his side .... "Just as many grains of wheat are used to make flour, and many grapes to make wine, many others will come together to form the kingdom on this earth .... Be patient with others, for they too shall recognize me through you .... Is there more that I can do for you?" .... I will leave you alone to talk to Jesus. Listen to his words of love. (*Pause.*)

Prayer

Jesus, I thank you for the comfort of your love. Give me strength when I am weak, faith when I doubt, and courage in the face of adversity. Amen.

It is time to leave the garden .... As a sign of faith, invite Jesus to place his hands upon your head in a blessing .... The warmth of unity in Christ spreads throughout your body and soul .... Say your good-byes for now .... Walk through the garden gate .... Run down the path with wings on your heels .... Open your eyes and return to this room.

Prayer Time

Invite the neophytes to share:

"What did you see? What did you feel?"

Dim the lights, lighting only one candle. Break off a piece of bread, pass it to the person next to you, then invite the neophytes to share the bread with each other, offering this prayer, "Jesus is the Bread of Life, (name)."

Pray the following:

Response: Lord, you are the Bread of Life.

Leader: Dear Jesus, we pray for those who have lost hope, that they will find you.

Response

Leader: We pray for those who have found the path to you, that they shall remain steadfast in their quest.

Response

Leader: We pray for our families that we may be able to build the kingdom of God within our homes.

Response

Leader: Bless us with courage to speak your name and serve our community.

Shepherd Me, O God

Scripture: Jn 10:1–10; Jn 10:11–18; Jn 10:27–30
Feast: 4th Sunday of Easter (ABC)
Music Suggestion: "Shepherd Me, O God"/*Instruments of Peace*

We are asked to look at our own spiritual gifts to discern their presence and the strength of each. We are asked to do this to be better able to serve the Lord, our shepherd. Recognizing Jesus as our shepherd may indeed be easier than defining our own gifts of the Spirit.

Can you picture yourself as a member of the priesthood or as performing deeds for the good of all mankind? Our most frequent cop-out is, "I think the Holy Spirit passed right by me" or better, "What can I do? I am only an amateur." Does the word *amateur* mean "laity" in your vernacular?

Small Groups

Read aloud 1 Cor 12:4–11.

Break into small groups for sharing and affirmation. It would be helpful for you and other volunteers to be ready with words of affirmation for the individual neophytes. The best way to do this is to have one facilitator in each group.

Invite each person to answer one question at a time around the group and why they may feel the way they do. Remember, there are no wrong and no right answers; this is the way they see themselves. The facilitator will go last, listing the gifts they see present in each one.

- If the gift of wisdom is reached by having an open mind, learning from your own mistakes and those of others, and having a firm grip on the meaning of life and a relationship with God, how would you rate yourself from 1 to 5, with 5 being the highest? Why?

- Do you have the ability to express your gift of knowledge with love and compassion to others? What ministries might this serve?

- Describe a recent experience in which the Holy Spirit blessed you with the gift of faith.

- If the gift of healing included not only miraculous healings due to professional care but also compassion and the ability to bring joy where there is sadness, order in the midst of chaos, and the ability to heal an aching heart, how would you rate yourself on a scale of 1 to 5?

- If the gift of tongues were defined as speaking the language of the Holy Spirit, using love and compassion to communicate and offering words of encouragement rather than ridicule, how do you rate?

- If the gift of interpretation of tongues were to be defined as the ability to *listen* to others, to *hear their words*, not your own, do you feel you have received this gift? Why or why not?

Ask each group to pray for one another and the reception of the gifts of the Spirit.

Meditation

Read aloud Jn 10:11–18.

Jesus addresses the importance of recognizing himself as our shepherd and ourselves as sheep, responding with eagerness at the sound of his voice. All three cycles of the Lectionary relate this concept. Recognizing Jesus as our shepherd helps us to understand that Jesus will keep us safe and will bless us with every gift of the Spirit, and all of our worldly needs. Let us join our Lord, Jesus.

Find a comfortable position .... Close your eyes .... Shut out the sights and sounds of the day .... Allow your body to relax .... Take a deep breath .... Let it out slowly. Whisper "Jesus" ....

You are in a grassy field, far away from the city. The land is rough .... Huge rocks jut out of the earth .... It is early evening .... Sheep and their lambs graze on the last blades of grass .... A tiny black lamb walks over to you .... Bend over and pet him .... Feel the softness of the lamb's wool .... Sense his trust in you .... A voice calls out from beyond the trees .... "The lamb thinks you are his shepherd" .... Look into the rays of the setting sun .... The figure moving toward you is only a shadow .... You recognize his voice; it is Jesus! .... He calls you by name .... "Watch out for that little lamb, he will wander off," Jesus cautions .... He is smiling and happy .... "Come and sit with me for a while" .... Hand in hand you and Jesus walk to the shade of a small clump of trees ....

The little lamb curls up in your lap, resting in your warmth .... The cool of evening fills the air with mist .... Jesus leans forward and pats the little guy, "You are being a good shepherd, you know. I'm going to tell you a true story that will help you to understand what I expect of you. Always use the gifts of the Spirit to help you discern a need .... Listen to the voice of others, know their hearts as I know my sheep ....

"If the lambs tire, a good shepherd will carry them, just as I will always walk with you." Jesus reaches down and pets the tiny lamb. You settle back against Jesus' arm ....

"There is a shepherd who lives in Oregon to this day. His name is William .... For many years William worked hard protecting his sheep from wolves and coyotes and intruders .... He raised his family amidst the beauty of the forest and rivers. William knew the gifts that were bestowed upon him and served God in every way that he could .... William thought that he knew everything there was to know about being a shepherd ....

"At long last he saved enough money to buy a little farm. He planted a garden and purchased some cows and chickens. His beloved sheep grazed in his front yard, protected in the evening hours and long Oregon rains by a ramshackle barn.

William worried about his animals during storms and heavy snows .... But on this night the storm came as a sudden visitor to the valley, racking the land with rain and hail the size of golf balls. William quickly went to the barn, shooing the last of his animals into the old red structure .... Once inside his house and safe from the ravages of the storm, William heard the bleating of a lamb. He went outside to find a lamb lying on the frozen ground. The lamb was shaking and quivering. When it thundered, the lamb shook harder. William picked the lamb up, dried it off, held it for a short time, and then sent it on its way to the barn once again ....

"Later in the evening, William went out to feed the animals. In the darkness, he tripped over a small figure lying on the porch. Bending down he discovered the body of the little lamb—scared to death by the storm .... The lamb had sought the protection of his shepherd. William, though caring and thoughtful, had failed this little lamb in his time of need .... William is a good man and today he is a much better shepherd. He did not realize how much the lamb needed the safety of his arms and the warmth of his home ....

"To this day, tears cloud William's eyes when he tells this story. He tells everyone, "I should have held him a little longer, until he felt safe. I just needed to give a little more of my time" ....

Jesus leans forward, rubbing his hands to keep warm. "This is a sad story but one that we all should be familiar with .... I will always protect and love you. I will never leave you alone. I will always know the sound of your voice .... In the days to come you, too, will be asked to shepherd others on their journey of faith. I ask only that you offer them all the time and energy that it takes to keep them safe and to feel loved. My love shall shine in you, leading others into the light" ....

You smile at Jesus, feeling safe and secure .... Jesus looks into your eyes, beyond your being, and asks, "Is there someone or something in your life that needs 'just a little more time'?" ....
I will leave you alone with Jesus, your good shepherd.

Prayer

Jesus, allow me to feel the strength of the Holy Spirit, accepting the gifts as they are bestowed upon me. May I serve others as you serve me. Open my ears to your call. Amen.

Discussion

• If you could give just "a little more time" to someone or something in your life, who or what would that be?

Closing Prayer

Gather in a circle. Light a candle. Invite the neophytes to think of someone who has taken "a little more time" with them, a good shepherd, who they in turn would like to bless in a special way.

Leader: Jesus, we ask you to bless (*name*).

Response: Thank you, Jesus, for sending this shepherd into my life.

Pray the Our Father.

Sweet Harvest
Of His Love

Scripture: Jn 14:1–12; Jn 15:1–17; Jn 13:31–33,34–35
Feast: 5th Sunday of Easter (ABC)
Music Suggestion: any selection from *Dream Journey*
     or "When You Seek Me"/*Gentle Sounds*

People gathered to hear Jesus speak because he spoke about situations that they could understand. He was concerned that they understand his meaning and could then incorporate it into their own lives. Many of his followers were shepherds or worked in vineyards; some were farmers. The people could relate to his stories. Can we?

Jesus speaks to our hearts as well. Within the pages of all three lectionary cycles, his instructions leave his imprint on our lives. In Cycle A Jesus reminds us that there are many paths to God, "My Father's house has many rooms; I will prepare a place for you." Cycle B finds us standing among the vineyard workers, pruning away the dead branches from the vine and gathering in the sweet harvest of love. In Cycle C, he will assemble us once more to teach us yet another definition of the word *love*—one that we should carry in our hearts all the days of our lives.

Let us release our imaginations, going back in time to the days of our Lord. Jesus will speak to your heart.

Meditation

Find a comfortable position .... Close your eyes .... Roll your shoulders back and forth, releasing the tension .... Relax ....

Shut out the cares and noises of the day …. Take a deep
breath …. Let it out slowly. Whisper "Jesus" ….

Once again we make our visit during Passover …. You enter a
small crowded room …. Jesus sits on the floor with his
disciples. Pillows soften the rough-hewn planks …. The table
is cluttered with cups and bowls …. Food remains on the
serving platters …. A half-eaten loaf of bread and a goblet of
wine sit on the table in front of Jesus, a drop of red wine falls
from the rim of the cup, etching its way across the table
linens ….

Paul leans forward, beckoning for you to join them around the
table …. Jesus looks up and smiles as you take your place
beside Philip …. Philip's young smooth skin stands out in
contrast to that of Peter, the fisherman …. Thomas, leaning
across the narrow table, whispers, "Jesus says that he is going
to be leaving us, but we don't know why or where he is
going" …. Abruptly, Jesus announces, "I am the way, and the
truth, and the life; no one comes to the Father, except
through me. If you know me, you will know my Father, also"
(Jn 14:6–7) …. Absentmindedly, Thomas muses, "How can
we follow him if we don't know how to get there?" …. A voice
rings out in answer, "One step at a time, one step at a time,
my friend" …. Jesus continues …. "I will not abandon you like
ships at sea. The disciples murmur, talking among
themselves …. Jesus strikes the side of a cup sharply with a
spoon. "I have much to tell you; allow me this precious time to
speak" ….

Pointing to the goblet of wine, Jesus asks, "My friend, if you
were the branch of the vine that produced these grapes, and
the gardener approached with a knife to cut you free of the
vine, would you be pleased?" …. Words stick in your
mouth …. Nod your head, thinking about the results of this
drastic action …. Jesus reaches over the table, placing his
hand on your head, "I am the real vine, and my Father is the
gardener. Every barren branch of mine he cuts away; and
every fruiting branch he cleans, in order to have larger

crops .... God has tended you well by pruning you back for greater usefulness and strength" ....

You give thought to what this has to do with you but you remain seated in silence .... Paul rests his head in his hands, deep in thought .... Jesus rises from the table .... He walks the length of the room, "Dwell in me, as I in you. No branch can bear fruit by itself, but only if it remains united with the vine" .... You feel puzzled .... Jesus, noticing your expression, turns his attention directly to you .... He lets out a deep sigh, walking across the room as though a burden is upon his shoulders .... He kneels by your side .... The disciples are busy talking among themselves .... Jesus speaks to you alone. "Sit with me, my friend" .... Slowly lowering himself to a small fireside stool, he pats the hearth next to him. You take your seat, leaning against the stone wall .... Tying his long hair behind his neck, Jesus begins, "My child, there are those things which you must not forget. Carry their truths with you all the days of your life .... One day we shall meet again in my Father's house. As you are a part of me, I am part of my Father. To know me is to know the face of God .... So shall others see the reflection of God in you" .... "But" you stammer .... Jesus places a finger over your lips ....

"As I have told my disciples, there are many paths to God's house. Do not ridicule the efforts of others on this journey .... Rest in me, for I am the way, the truth, and the life of all that has been and all that will be" .... Gently, he brushes your hair away from your face, "Remain in me, spread my love to others. I am the vine and you the branches. As the vine cannot bear fruit apart from the vine, so, too, shall you be. Go forth into the world bearing much fruit .... Remember, you did not choose me. I chose you and appoint you to go and bear fruit—fruit that will last—love one another" ....

Rising, he takes your hands in his, "Friend, do you understand that apart from me you can do nothing?" .... Jesus pauses, then asks, "Are there things in your life that need to be cut away? (Pause.) Is there time for me in your world? (Pause.)

I will leave you alone with Jesus for a few minutes. Open your mind and your heart to him.

Prayer

My Lord, my God, fill me with your Spirit. Open my eyes to your truth. Open my heart, allowing the fruit of your love to ripen within me. Allow me the grace to offer love rather than condemnation. Thank you, Lord. Amen.

Discussion

Form small groups.

- What did you see? What did you hear?
- If God were to appear as your gardener, what would he do with you?
- On those days that you feel cut off from the "vine" and everything is going wrong, what do you do to get in touch again?

Closing

In your small groups spend a few minutes in reflection on sharing Jesus' command to "love one another" when it comes to your own family. Are there problems? Are there blessings? Invite the groups to offer a short prayer—a word of thanks or request. Form a large group when completed. Join hands and pray the Lord's Prayer.

I Will Come Back To You

Scripture: Jn 14:23–29
Feast: 6th Sunday of Easter (C)
Music Suggestion: any selection from *Dream Journey*
** or "I Will Never Forget You"/*Gentle Sounds***

Jesus knew that loving others would be very difficult at times for us so he promised to send us a Paraclete to strengthen and guide us. A Paraclete is someone who stands beside us when we have a difficult action to take, giving us courage and support. The Paraclete, in this case, is the Holy Spirit. The Holy Spirit is like the breath of God, clearing away doubt and fear, leaving in its path the love and surety of God.

Before Jesus died, he promised his followers that the Holy Spirit would always be with us. But, following his death, doubt and fears clouded the apostles' minds. Let us join the disciples once again in the crowded upstairs room to experience the Peace of Jesus.

Meditation

This evening finds us sitting in silence in the darkened upper room. The windows are boarded shut .... The air is heavy and stale .... One tiny candle dimly filters the darkness .... It is like a bad dream; everyone is caught in the shadows .... They speak in hushed voices .... His head in his hands, Peter sobs quietly, "My friend, my Lord, has abandoned me" .... Place your hand on Peter's shoulder .... Feel his sadness .... Tears form in your eyes .... A man's shadow is cast on the wall .... Turn around .... It is Jesus! .... He places his hand above your

head, "Don't be afraid, my friend. May my peace be with
you" .... The room brightens with the light of Christ .... Your
burdens fade .... Your worries disappear and your tears turn
to a soft smile .... Jesus quickly moves among the disciples,
reassuring them that he will never leave them alone to face
life's hardships .... Peter collapses at his feet in shame and
sorrow .... Jesus takes Peter's rough calloused hands into his,
helping him to his feet, "I love you, Peter" .... Turning to the
others, he speaks once again .... "Where two or three are
gathered in my name, I am with you. You will never be alone
again. My Father is going to send the Holy Spirit who will
teach you everything and remind you of all that I have said" ....

Jesus walks through the crowded room stopping to reach out
and touch those whose arms and hands reach toward him. A
feeling of well-being and safety spreads throughout .... At last
he walks to where you are standing, your back touching a
darkened corner of the room. Bending on one knee he calls
you by name, "Never be afraid my dear friend. Let your heart
be at peace. I promise you that you will never stand alone
again. I will always be with you" .... Warmth, love, and an
awareness of the hardships of others fill your heart .... Slowly
Jesus surrounds you with his arms, and whispers, "Recognize
these feelings of love. Let them take root in your heart" ....
Holding you close, he adds, "I love you" .... Bask in his
warmth for a moment. (*Pause briefly.*) Jesus continues, "I
know that it is not always easy to love your enemies. It is not
always easy to love members of your own family, let alone the
homeless who stand dirty and soiled on the street corners, and
yet I ask this of you" .... Jesus casts his eyes about the room,
"The Holy Spirit shall be your guide through a sometimes
godless world. I ask only that you obey my commands, resolve
to turn the other cheek in times of adversity, and to do good
for those who persecute you. Allow my Holy Spirit to show
you the way" .... Quiet and peace surround you .... I will give
you a few minutes to talk to Jesus. Speak to him from your
heart ....

Prayer

Jesus, at times I grow calloused and hardened to your "nudge" to offer your love and peace to others. I become absorbed in fearing what others may think of me. I don't spend enough time with you. For all the times it is difficult for me to act in loving ways—fill me with your Spirit, Jesus. May your command to love become the cornerstone of my faith. May I live in your peace forever. Amen.

The light of dawn ends the ghostly shadows of night .... It is now time for you to make your way quietly down the back stairway .... Glance back once more, then walk out into the early morning mist .... Open your eyes and return to this room.

Discussion

- Share a time in your life when you felt the presence of the Holy Spirit—perhaps a time when fear overwhelmed you, only to be replaced with the strength you needed.
- When is it the most difficult for you to show others the peace of Christ?

Prayer Service

Supplies: Bible opened to John 14:23–29, a large candle, background music or "Come Holy Spirit"/"In the Spirit We Belong"

Lower the lights. Invite the neophytes to take a few minutes in silence to reflect on one person in their life who they find it difficult to love. Ask the Holy Spirit to help you love the unlovable. Form a circle around the lighted candle. Read from the Bible, first raising it reverently above your head then returning it to a place of honor.

Leader: May the world become a more peaceful place where people learn to forgive. May the world be filled with the joy of the Lord when we take time to enjoy the presence of others. May we extend the love of Christ

169

to those we find unlovable. Open our eyes and our hearts to the peace of our Lord.

Invite everyone to offer a sign of peace to each other: "May the Peace of the Lord be with you always."

Close with the Lord's Prayer.

As God Sent Me, I Send You Into the World

Scripture: Jn 17:1–11; Jn 17:11–19; Jn 17:20–26
Feast: 7th Sunday of Easter (ABC)
Music Suggestion: "Only a Shadow"/*Gentle Sounds*

Scripture scholars believe the Gospel according to John is his focus or meditation on the meaning of the life and ministry of Jesus. The simplicity of John's words tell of the birth of Jesus into a world to give glory to his Father and eternal life to his believers. Having selected and trained his disciples, Jesus needed to fulfill the Scriptures of old. Upon his death, the world of believers would know life everlasting. With this accomplished, he returned to his Father, leaving this message of hope with his followers who in turn would share the Good News of God.

Nearing the day of Pentecost, we find ourselves about to take on the role of apostle. The word *apostle* comes from the Greek meaning "one who is sent." There is a distinction between the use of the word *disciple* and that of *apostle*. Simply put, *disciple* means "student," or one who is learning. *Apostle* indicates the student has learned his/her lessons well and now it is time "to be sent out." Let's spend a few moments reflecting upon the words of prayer Jesus offered his Father in Heaven.

Meditation

Find a comfortable position .... Close your eyes .... Shut away
the sounds and trials of today .... Relax, allow your arms to
feel limp .... Take a deep breath .... Let it out slowly ....
Whisper "Jesus" ....

It is the evening of the final Passover meal .... Once again you
sit on pillows around a long, roughly hewn table .... All are
present, except one .... Jesus speaks of leaving .... He speaks
of death .... He speaks of promises .... Peter interrupts, not
grasping the truths .... Jesus seems pensive, impatient with
the lack of knowledge—perhaps frustrated by reality ....

The low murmur of voices stops as Jesus stands among the
men, raising his voice in prayer to signal the evening drawing
to a close .... Listen to his words .... "I gave them the words
you gave me and they accepted them. They believed that you
sent me .... I pray for them. I remain in the world no longer.
Protect them by the power of your name" .... Falling to his
knees, he pleads, "Sanctify them by your truth; your word is
truth. As you sent me into the world, I have sent them into the
world .... I pray for all those who will believe in me through
their message. May the world come to live in unity through
their belief in me. Amen" .... Jesus drops his arms, exhaustion
covers his face .... You see the reflection of pain and torment
in his eyes; clearly, he knows his fate ....

"Come, my friend, rest with me," Jesus invites .... You follow
Jesus out into the night .... Whispers hide in the shadows ....
The end of life lies near .... The beginning of life lies in the
hope of a rising sun .... "Kneel before me, child," Jesus
orders .... Instantly, you drop before him, unsure of your
role .... Jesus places his hands, palms down, upon the top of
your head .... He speaks only to you in these closing hours of
life .... "I have come to bring glory to my Father .... Through
your work, God's name shall also be glorified. Love binds me
to Father God .... Christians must be bound together in love
and unity. I ask this of you" ....

Jesus leans ever so slightly forward, causing gentle pressure
upon your head—perhaps a reminder of the importance of

172

what he asks of you .... "Rise, my child, prepare to go into the world. Carry my words upon your lips, my love within your heart .... Bring my message of unity to your world " .... You stutter, falling backward two steps. "Why me, Lord?" .... Your silent question does not go unnoticed .... "Because I love you, my child," Jesus responds.

I will give you a few minutes alone with Jesus .... Questions swirl in your mind .... Listen for the voice of your Lord. (*Pause.*)

Prayer

Jesus, I feel no less confused than your first disciples. Allow your will to be manifest in me. May I serve you as a student, always learning, and as your apostle. May your blessing fall upon my family, bringing them together in your name. Amen.

The evening hour has drawn to a close .... It is time to say good-bye for now .... Feel the warmth of Jesus' love .... Walk down the shadow-covered streets .... Open your eyes and return to this room.

Discussion

- How can you share Jesus' message of unity and love in your own home? in the office?
- How do you recognize another Christian?
- In what ways will it be comfortable for you to share your faith?

Closing Prayer

Holding hands, join in singing "They Will Know We Are Christians by Our Love." Close with the Lord's Prayer in echo format.

The Breath of Life

Scripture: Jn 20:19–23
Feast: Pentecost (ABC)
Music Suggestion: "Only a Shadow"/*Gentle Sounds*

When the gusty autumn winds send golden leaves scurrying across the yard, most of us realize it is the wind even though we cannot see it. We can only observe the action the wind causes. The soft gentle breeze of an electric fan on a summer evening can only be felt. The Holy Spirit is much like the movement of air, only to be experienced, not seen. The Holy Spirit gives us the courage and the strength to make the right decisions and to take the correct action. Jesus has promised the gift of the Holy Spirit to enable us to continue his work on earth, giving us the strength to walk with our Lord.

After Jesus' death, his friends were terrified, going and coming only at night. They gathered together waiting and hoping that Jesus would once again appear. Let us release our imaginations to join his disciples in the upper room to experience the coming of the Holy Spirit.

Darken the room, lighting one small candle. Ask a helper to stand among the group, greeting them with "Peace be with you!"

Meditation

Find a comfortable position .... Tense your body for several seconds, then relax your head and your neck .... Now, your back .... Your arms feel limp, falling into a comfortable position .... Take a deep breath .... Let it out slowly ....

It is nightfall .... Darkness begins to cover the day with its shadows .... You are moving through the darkened streets, looking first to the right and then to the left .... No one is following you .... Slowly, quietly, make your way up the creaking stairway .... At last, Peter opens the door to a small darkened room ....

Candles flicker .... Shadows dance across the crowded room, bouncing off the frightened faces .... The door creaks behind you .... Three more people come into the room .... The air is heavy and stale .... The windows are boarded shut .... People speak in soft whispers, hoping the night air will not carry the sound of their voices to the streets far below ....

You recognize Mary, the mother of Jesus .... She sits quietly, waiting by the door; half expecting, half knowing the presence of Jesus .... A tear glistens in the candlelight .... John stands closely by, his hand on her shoulder .... Walk over to Mary .... Wrap your arms about her shoulders .... Take a moment to speak to the mother of your Lord. (*Pause.*)

A knock on the door shatters the quiet .... Move to a darkened corner of the room .... Peter cautiously opens the door .... James makes his way into the room. "The Roman soldiers are searching the houses for us. We need to observe extra caution this night" .... Peter moves to the light of a candle, a rough red beard frames his face, "If only Jesus were here ... " .... His words hang in the air .... Without warning, the sound of surging winds fills the room, reminding you of the whistling sound of wind whipping through treetops .... The whole house shakes beneath your feet .... Doors rattle .... Boards on the windows break, setting the hurricane winds free .... The candles and lanterns flicker, then die .... You feel the gust rushing through your hair .... Before you can move or speak, a subdued light fills the room .... Bright lights in the shape of flames rest upon each head .... Looking up, you see the tongues of fire above your own head ....

No longer do you feel fear .... a calm settles over everyone in the room .... Peace covers you like a warm blanket on a cold winter's night .... Happiness and joy flow from your toes and up through your heart .... So many feelings fill you—the

lightness of a spring day, the excitement of Christmas ....
Enjoy the moment—fears are gone; strength is renewed ....

"It is the Spirit of God!" Peter shouts .... In his usual calm,
John whispers, "Jesus kept his promise" .... People move
about the room joyfully, laughing, dancing .... Peter takes your
hands and leads you to the center of the room .... "Feel joy,
my friend. The Spirit of the Lord is truly with you!" .... Nearly
knocked off balance, you feel the warm breath of God rush
through you ....

The windows and doors stand open .... Rush down the stairs
into the starlit night .... Dancing and laughter fill the street ....
Strength firms your convictions to share your Jesus experience
with others .... Feel the freedom from fear .... Within your
heart lies the peace of the Lord ....

Take a moment to ask the Holy Spirit to guide you in your life
choices .... To experience the love of God .... And the ability
to show love to the lovable and the unlovable. (*Pause.*)

Prayer

*Jesus, bless me with the strength of my convictions,
the faith to live by, and the gentleness of your love.
May the Holy Spirit dwell within my heart and with
this community. Amen.*

It is time to leave now .... Wave good-bye to those gathered in
the square .... Remember, the Holy Spirit is within your soul
when you choose to love and to share your happiness and
peace .... Make your way down the cobblestone street ....
Open your eyes and return to this room.

Discussion

*Form small groups to share their responses to each
question. Complete the first question before going on to
the second.*

- What did you see? What did you hear?
- Share a time in your life when you have been aware of the
  presence of the Holy Spirit.

Closing Prayer

Recite the words of the Apostles' Creed together; close with Glory Be.

Music Resources

Background music for guided meditations is readily available from both religious and secular stores. Listen for music that can set a mood, usually peaceful, but does not call attention to itself. I have found that using a background of nature sounds combined with music is the most effective choice. This type of music provides a relaxing environment, not causing group members to "turn off" because of an improper music selection. Here are some of my favorites.

Bamboo Waterfall. Northwood Music. A combination of music and nature sounds, wind chimes, bells, waterfalls, wind, waves, and streams.

Darnell, Dik. *Ceremony*. Etherean Music. Beautiful instrumentals that work well with the meditations.

Fitzgerald, Scott. *Dreamland*. Northwood Music. Gentle music blends calming sounds of waves, rain, crickets, and other nature sounds.

Haugen, Marty. *Instruments of Peace*. GIA.

Landry, Carey. *Gentle Sounds*. NALR. This album works well with the meditations. The music is arranged so that you are able to cross from one piece to the next without disrupting the meditation.

Richard, Gary. *Dream Journey*. Northwood Music. Blends soft, dreamy music with soothing natural sounds.

———. *Water Music*. Northwood Music. Guitar and nature's most eloquent instrument—water.

The Sea. Northwood Music. Waves on sandy beaches, crashing waves, tide pools, seagulls, just sounds of nature. These are very effective and relaxing.

Thunderstorms. Northwood Music. The rush of wind, rolling thunder, heavy rainfall, very dramatic.

Winston, George. *December*. Windham Hill Productions.

Resources for Liturgical Catechesis

GUIDED MEDITATIONS FOR TEENS
Living Through the Church Year

Sydney Ann Merritt

Paper, 192 pages, 5½" x 8½", ISBN: 0-89390-402-3

Meditative prayer through Scripture offers the student easy access to Jesus, his life and times. These 41 meditations, based on the church year, will guide your teenagers to a deeper relationship with Jesus. The teens will be led into a Gospel scene where they will encounter the Lord through touch, feel, love and prayer. They will "hear" the brush of angel wings, experience the wonderment of the day of Pentecost, and "feel" the raging sea plummet the fishing boat they share with Jesus. The book is designed to be a personal experience; however, questions or activities follow each meditation to help build Christian community.

GUIDED MEDITATIONS FOR CHILDREN
40 Scripts and Activities Based on the Sunday Lectionary

Sydney Ann Merritt

Paper, 192 pages, 5½" x 8½", ISBN: 0-89390-336-1

These 40 guided meditations are all related to the Sunday lectionary with accompanying prayers, discussion questions, and related activities. The book includes tips on how to do guided meditations that work every time. Pick the one you want, adapt it, or read it as is.

STORIES FOR CHRISTIAN INITIATION

Joseph J. Juknialis

Paper, 152 pages, 6" x 9", ISBN: 0-89390-235-7

This collection of 11 stories is organized around the adult catechumenate. These are not allegories; they are imaginative stories that resonate with key lectionary passages and stages of the catechumenate. Great for generating discussions. Reflections, questions, and rituals for each story will help catechumens tell their own stories.

RCIA SPIRITUALITY
Formation for the Catechumenate Team

Barbara Hixon with Reflection Questions by Gael Gensler, OSF

Paper, 192 pages, 5½" x 8½", ISBN: 0-89390-399-X

The catechumenal process is not something you do to someone else. It's something that happens to you, the team member, as much as to the catechumen. The authors show you how each step of the catechumenate process will change your life. Gael Gensler's questions help turn this book into a useful group formation tool for your team.

Resources for Liturgical Catechesis

EUCHARIST
An Eight-Session Ritual-Catechesis Experience for Adults

Susan S. Jorgensen

Paper, 200 pages, 8½" x 11", ISBN: 0-89390-293-4

Participants in this eight-week program work through the prayers of the Eucharistic liturgy, from opening rite to dismissal, and emerge with deep understanding of the words and gestures of the Eucharist. This could be the mystagogia experience you've been looking for, or the way to help your liturgical ministers understand the heart and soul of the liturgy.

"Susan Jorgensen has created a living, breathing, working process for community transformation... respectful of differences, open to the variety of approaches, ready to use and well designed, it is a strong resource and strong spark to our ritual imaginations."
　　　　 – Catholic Press Association Book Award Judges

A BOOK OF RITUAL PRAYERS
30 Celebrations for Parishes, Schools, and Faith Communities

Jerry Welte and Marlene Kemper Welte

Paper, 160 pages, 5½" x 8½", ISBN: 0-89390-397-3

"The liturgies in this book are admirable models of what celebration is all about. These rituals engage the heart and the head and all five senses in creative ways which will stimulate the imagination of anyone who works with liturgy. This is a practical book which teaches us, through marvelous examples, how to think about what we are celebrating and how to go about planning that celebration, step by step." 　　　 — Tad Guzie, Professor of Education at the University of Calgary

CATECHIZING WITH LITURGICAL SYMBOLS
25 Hands-on Sessions for Teens and Adults

Pamela J. Edwards

Paper, 128 pages, 8½" x 11", ISBN: 0-89390-401-5

You know the power of symbols. The power to inspire. To enrich. To deepen faith. But most resources on symbols are dry, wordy, theoretical treatises. Not this one. Here's a practical, 25-session program for expanding family understanding and sensitivity for symbols. In these sessions, people interact with these symbols, are touched by them, and let them become a part of their faith experience. The examples included in this work can be done at home, in the classroom or with a worship environment, all with a minimum of aesthetic training and only a small investment in time or money.

Order these books from your local bookseller or call:
1-888-273-7782 (toll free) or 1-408-286-8505
or visit the web site at www.rpinet.com